Classical Liberalism

by
Charles Siegel

Preservation
Institute

Cover: Jean Leon Gerome Ferris (1863–1930)
"Writing the Declaration of Independence, 1776"

Text copyright © 2011 by Charles Siegel
Published by the Preservation Institute, Berkeley, California
www.preservenet.com

Contents

Chapter 1 The Lost Liberal Tradition 5
   Classical, Victorian, and Modernist Liberalism 7
   Positive and Negative Freedom 11
   Beyond Modernism 13

Chapter 2 In Search of Classical Liberalism 17
   Liberalism in Greece and Rome 18
   Liberalism in the Middle Ages and After 31
   Moral Individualism 48

Chapter 3 Two Faces of Victorian Liberalism 56
   Industrialization and Politics 58
   Liberalism and Self-Interest 64
   Liberalism and Idealism 75
   Victorian Hypocrisy 89

Chapter 4 Modernist Liberalism 93
   The Consumer Economy 95
   Modernist Philosophy 105
   From Idealism to Modernism 117

Chapter 5 Personal Freedom in the Courts 122
   Religion as Personal Behavior 124
   Loitering as Freedom of Assembly 127
   Freedom of Speech to Freedom of Expression 131
   Modernism and Powerlessness 137
   Liberals Move Beyond Modernism 138

Chapter 6 After Modernism 143
   Individual Choice 147
   Political Choice 170
   Reducing Inequality 178

Chapter 7 The Future of Liberalism 182
   Our Conceptual Blind Spot 183
   A New Direction 190
   Negative or Positive Freedom 195

Notes 200

Chapter 1
The Lost Liberal Tradition

Conventional historians say that liberalism went through two historical stages, which we can call laissez-faire liberalism and modernist liberalism.

In this view, liberalism began as a defense of the early capitalist economy, which was made up primarily of small, independent businesses. The early version of liberalism focused on individual freedom, on the free market, and on limited government – a laissez-faire theory that was useful to promote economic growth in the days when independent entrepreneurs were hampered by government controls and by mercantile monopolies. The political ideal of individual freedom was based on the economic ideal of individual freedom.

In this view, liberal political theory began in the seventeenth century, in the early days of the rise of capitalism. Thomas Hobbes, John Locke and others argued that individuals naturally pursue their self-interest and that they institute government by creating a social contract to protect themselves from other individuals with conflicting self-interests. It follows that government power is legitimate only to the extent that it serves this purpose. Economic theory of the eighteenth and nineteenth century supported this political theory: Adam Smith and other economists showed that a nation is most prosperous if there is minimum government interference in individuals' pursuit of their self-interest.

Nineteenth century liberals, like today's libertarians, called for minimum government interference in the freedom to pursue one's own interests – both economic freedom and personal freedom. The focus on self-interest reflected the realities of the market economy that thrived from the sixteenth to the nineteenth century. Though Hobbes believed in authoritarian government, he is often called a founder of liberalism, because he was the first modern thinker to argue that government was founded to protect individuals' self-interest.[1]

In this view, a new form of liberalism emerged in the twentieth century, as the early capitalist economy of independent businesses was being replaced by a more centralized, more bureaucratized economy. Laissez-faire economics seemed to lead to monopoly that threatened competition, and laissez-faire no longer seemed to offer unlimited opportunity to anyone who started a business and worked hard. Early in the twentieth century, progressives began to emphasize the need for state intervention to protect ourselves from excessive corporate power and to give everyone the basics of a decent life, such as public education. There were many contradictory strands to the liberalism of the early twentieth century, but after laissez-faire was discredited by the Great Depression, a new version of liberalism emerged during the late New Deal and in post-war America, which was based on the idea that the government must fine-tune the economy to promote stability and growth and must provide entitlement programs to ensure that everyone has a fair share of the prosperity that economic growth generates.[2]

Modernist liberals no longer believed in free enterprise, but they still believed in personal freedom, as nineteenth-century liberals had. They continued to be groups: civic republicans in self-governing cities such as Florence, who emphasized the importance of civic virtue, and radical Protestants, such as the Anabaptists and the Quakers, who emphasized freedom of conscience. Civic republican and radical Protestant ideas fused in England in the mid seventeenth century, at the time of the Puritan commonwealth, to form a classical liberal ideal that remained important at the time of the American revolution. This classical liberalism was based on moral individualism, which was very different from the self-interested individualism of laissez-faire liberalism.

Adding classical liberalism to the conventional history of liberalism lets us make more sense of early American political history: We can see that early American politics involved a clash between classical liberalism and the commercial liberalism that followed.

When America was founded, the Jeffersonians were in this classical liberal tradition. They went a step further than earlier classical liberals, because they recognized that economic changes had undermined freedom in the past: They wanted to limit the economy so people could continue to run their own small farms and small businesses, because they believed that this economic independence developed the character needed for democratic self-government. In their view, freedom meant that people had the right to make serious decisions about how society was run – both small decisions about running their own business affairs and larger political decisions about running their communities.

When America was founded, the Federalists stood for economic growth and for a newer commercial version of liberalism, based on self-interested individualism. Their policies were meant to promote trade and manufacturing, and they were more interested in economic prosperity than strong supporters of civil liberties even though they supported more government control over the economy.

Classical, Victorian and Modernist Liberalism

I began to research this book because I was dissatisfied with this conventional history of liberalism, with its two stages of laissez-faire and modernism. This history seemed to diminish liberalism by interpreting it as a reaction to transient economic circumstances. Liberalism includes deeper and more permanent human ideals than this – such as self-government, freedom of thought, and freedom of conscience. These ideals emerged earlier in history than the conventional theory can account for – freedom of thought and self-government in classical Athens and freedom of conscience among the radical Protestant sects.

I found that there was another version of liberalism that preceded the two versions of the conventional history, which we can call classical liberalism. This earliest form of liberalism appeared at times when subsistence agricultural economies based on traditional methods were first being replaced by economies of independent small farmers and small craftsmen in self-governing communities, but it tended to be eclipsed after a short time, as these economies were replaced by economies dominated by trade. I found that we tend to overlook classical liberalism because it usually flourished so briefly that it produced little or no political theory.

Nevertheless, it is possible to write the history of classical liberalism. It has its roots in antiquity, in Athens and Rome, with the beginning of free thought, republican self-government, and an independent civil society. After the Middle Ages, classical liberalism was revived by two in civic virtue. This is the bias that conventional historians now consider the earliest form of liberalism, but it was actually the newer strand of liberalism at the time of the American revolution.

Adding classical liberalism to the conventional history also lets us make more sense of later American history. We can see that there was another side to the American liberalism of the later nineteenth century that continued the moral liberalism of the Jeffersonians and that was very different from self-interested laissez-faire liberalism. This other side of nineteenth century liberalism was responsible for many of the most important social advances of the nineteenth and early twentieth century: Abolitionists and feminists generally were motivated primarily by this idealistic side of liberalism and not by laissez faire – many of them inspired by Emerson's idealism – and this other side of liberalism remained influential in the civil rights movement of the mid-twentieth century.

There was a sharp distinction in later nineteenth century America between liberal thinking about the economy and liberal thinking about social issues. By the 1840's, the Federalists had won the battle about the future of the economy, and Americans abandoned the Jeffersonians' resistance to economic modernization. Liberals accepted modernization and believed in laissez-faire economics, which is based on self-interest. The self-interested individualism that the conventional history considers the first phase of liberalism dominated American thinking about the economy during the Victorian period.

Yet the economy was still limited at this time. The business world was men's sphere. Women's sphere was home, church, and voluntary community organizations, which still had important social and economic functions at the time, and which were based on higher ideals than self-interest. When it came to economics, liberals believed in laissez faire, but abolitionists, feminists, and other liberal social reformers, who were often women, continued the older tradition of moral individualism inherited from classical liberalism.

Modernist liberalism displaced Victorian liberalism during the twentieth century, as the modern economy took over more and more of the functions of face-to-face groups. Liberals abandoned laissez faire and began to argue that big government should regulate big business to provide people with jobs, health care, education, retirement benefits, and so on, and at the same time, they came to believe that the modern economy had to be managed by planners who could make complex technical decisions that were beyond the understanding of most people. Ordinary people could no longer make the big decisions about how society is run, but modernist liberals maintained the long liberal commitment to freedom by promoting "personal freedom," freedom to act privately in ways that do not harm anyone else. For example, they wanted to eliminate what they called "victimless crimes" by legalizing any private behavior among consenting adults.

It is difficult to trace the history of liberalism, because the word "liberal" was not used in its current sense until the 1820s, and did not become common until decades later: Neither John Locke, nor Jefferson, nor Hamilton called themselves liberals.[3] But when we look at the origins of nineteenth and twentieth century liberal thought, we will see that the conventional history is wrong to say that liberalism passed through only two phases, laissez-faire and modernist liberalism.

Instead, it will become clear that liberalism has passed through three phases. Classical liberalism was based on moral individualism. Victorian liberalism had two faces: a new laissez-faire economic aspect based on self-interested individualism, and a social aspect that continued the classical tradition of moral individualism. Modernist liberalism was based on self-interested individualism.

During the nineteenth century, liberals still recognized that their politics was rooted in classical and radical protestant ideals. It is only during the twentieth century that liberals lost touch with the classical tradition so completely that they reinterpreted the history of liberalism to include nothing but laissez faire and modernism.

Positive and Negative Freedom

The word "liberal" comes from the Latin "liber," meaning free, but the liberal idea of freedom changed dramatically over the centuries, as the formal economy took over most of the work that people used to do independently and took over most of the decisions that people used to make for themselves.

Classical liberals believed in what has been called "positive freedom": Freedom means that you can make decisions about significant issues, such as managing your own business affairs, raising your own children, and helping to govern your own community.

By contrast, laissez-faire liberals and modernist liberals adopted a new idea of "negative freedom": Freedom means that the government does not interfere with your behavior.[4]

Liberals accommodated modernization by redefining freedom as negative. In nineteenth century America, the industrial revolution created a class of people who would never own their own farms or businesses and who would work for other people all their lives – something that shocked Americans in the 1830s and 1840s, when they first realized that it was happening. During the twentieth century, centralized organizations took over many responsibilities of families and voluntary groups. Once they accepted the ideal of negative freedom, liberals could live with the fact that modernization was making people more powerless: People still had their freedom, as long as they were free from direct government coercion.

As they shifted from positive to negative freedom, liberals rejected the moral bias of classical liberalism.

Classical liberals believed that a free nation had to be concerned with the character of its citizens, because people must rise above self-interest to govern themselves. Jeffersonians wanted to preserve an economy of small proprietors and farmers, precisely because they believed that managing their own businesses would help Americans develop the virtues that they needed as citizens. They believed that in Europe, industrialism was degrading workers by turning them into life-long employees, with a servile character that was incapable of self-government.

By contrast, laissez-faire liberals believed that government should be amoral: It should establish neutral rules that let people pursue their self-interest and that make people face the consequences of their decisions. Laissez-faire liberals invented what civic republican theorist Michael Sandel calls "the procedural republic,"[5] the idea that government should not promote any common idea of the good life but should simply enforce a set of fair rules that let individuals pursue their own interests.

Despite laissez faire, the older moral bias of liberalism remained important in Victorian America, among abolitionists, feminists, and other social reformers. At the beginning of the 1960s, moral liberalism still had some vitality left, and it was an important part of the anti-war movement, led by Quakers and by others grounded in religious traditions, and of the early civil rights movement led by Martin Luther King. This is the side of liberalism that gave it a reputation for idealism.

By the end of the 1960s, though, modernist liberalism had replaced moral liberalism almost entirely, as rapid post-war economic growth modernized virtually every aspect of life. Modernist liberals wanted the federal government to fine-tune the economy and to provide everyone with jobs, child care, education, and health care. At the same time, they carried the negative idea of personal freedom further than ever before: For example, they filed lawsuits defending loitering as a form of freedom of assembly and defending topless dancing as a form of freedom of speech.

The American Civil Liberties Union sometimes prevailed in the courts with these arguments, but most people decided that, if this was freedom, they wanted it in limited doses. Extreme forms of "personal freedom" helped to discredit the liberalism of the 1960s and 1970s and to lead the rise of Reaganite conservatism in the 1980s.

Because they focused on these negative freedoms, modernist liberals tended to ignore the much greater threat to freedom from a centralized economy that makes people powerless and dependent.

Beyond Modernism

The liberal ideal changed over the centuries to accommodate modernization. It must change again today, now that we are approaching the limits of modernization.

Modernist liberalism became popular in the early twentieth century by promising to bring the benefits of technology and economic growth to everyone. At a time when we had a scarcity economy, modernists appealed to a broad range of people by promising to promote economic prosperity and to use it to provide everyone with basic, decent housing, education, and health care.

But the modernist program no longer seems as attractive, now that we have moved from a scarcity economy to a surplus economy, where most people already have the basics. Once people already have enough, the promise of promoting economic growth rings hollow. It was one thing to promote economic growth in the early twentieth century to provide everyone with decent housing and education. It was something completely different to promote economic growth in the late twentieth century to provide everyone with bigger suburban homes, bigger SUVs and bigger freeways to drive them on.

Economic growth is no longer needed to provide most people with the basics, and we have also begun to realize that growth creates threats that no one dreamed of at the beginning of the twentieth century, such as global warming and depletion of fossil fuel supplies.

Classical liberal was eclipsed by laissez-faire and modernist liberalism because they accommodated the industrial revolution. As we move beyond the age of industrialization, the classical liberal tradition becomes relevant again. Of course, we are not going to move back to a Jeffersonian economy of independent small farms and small businesses. But we can revive the ideal of positive freedom by giving people significant choices about running their own lives. For example, we can let people choose to work part-time, so they have the option of working shorter hours and having more time for themselves, a right that employees already have in Germany and the Netherlands. Rather than spending more on health care, people could have more time to improve their own health by exercising. Rather than spending more on child care and after school programs, people could have more time to care for their own children. Rather than spending more on housing and transportation, people could live in walkable neighborhoods where they can get around on their own two feet.

Once people have enough, the classical liberal emphasis on virtue becomes important again, because we can do more to enhance our well-being by living well than we can by consuming more. For example, Americans spend twice as much per capita on health care as the other developing nations, but Americans have shorter life expectancy than the other developing nations. A large part of the problem is our epidemic of obesity, which causes type 2 diabetes, heart disease, and other diseases. We need to improve our health by adopting healthier habits, primarily by eating better and exercising more. And to do this, we need to realize that living healthy lives is more important that spending even more money on health care.[6]

Liberals must move beyond the old modernist policies that promote economic growth in order to provide people with more services, and instead must develop new policies that give people more positive freedom. We need to revive positive individual freedom, by developing social policies that give people more choices and more responsibilities. We also need to revive positive political freedom: Rather than abandoning economic decisions to the market and the government planners, we need to use the law to protect the public realm and to decide what sort of communities we live in.

Yet the ideal of positive freedom was eclipsed so completely by the ideal of negative freedom during two centuries of modernization that we have forgotten it almost completely. By looking at the history of Anglo-American liberalism and at how it changed in response to changing economic conditions, we can cast a new light on today's politics by rediscovering that classical liberal ideal.

Chapter 2
In Search of Classical Liberalism

It is hard to find examples of classical liberal thought, because free societies generally flourished for such short times that they produced little or no political philosophy. To reconstruct the classical liberal ideal, we must put the political philosophy that we do have into its historic context.

In ancient Greece and Rome and in medieval Europe, the rise of handicrafts production and small trade created an economy of small proprietors that bred free institutions, but as trade expanded, it created economic inequality that led to the rise of empires. By the time the Greeks and Romans began writing political philosophy, republics had either been discredited by class struggle or replaced by empire.

In the late middle ages, likewise, the rise of handicrafts production bred the free institutions of self-governing guilds and cities. Here, too, the rise of large-scale trade gave wealth and power to the old landowning classes: During the Renaissance, mercantilism led to rise of absolute monarchy and of empires.

But Renaissance Europe differed from classical Greece and Rome, because the urban economy was becoming more important than agriculture. Land owners controlled the empires of ancient times, but the commercial classes ultimately dominated government in Europe, because of their growing wealth. In England, for example, classical liberal thought flourished briefly at the time of the Puritan commonwealth – after the middle classes overthrew an absolute monarchy – but classical liberalism was soon replaced by the commercial liberalism of John Locke and of the laissez-faire economists, after the Restoration and the Glorious Revolution gave power to the wealthiest merchants and manufacturers.

Classical liberalism fell backward into monarchy ideals in ancient times, and it fell forward into commercial liberalism in modern times, but despite its short duration, we can find a core of ideals that define classical liberalism if we look at liberal thought in historic context. Classical liberals believed in positive freedom – both in democratic self-government, and in the freedom of individuals, families, and voluntary groups to act independently of the government. Classical liberals insisted that there should be a government of laws, not of men, and a division of powers among the branches of government to protect civil society from the tyranny of the majority – ideas that were a staple of political philosophy from Aristotle onward. Classical liberals also developed a theory of natural rights based on natural law, which was meant to protect positive freedom; this theory has been forgotten almost completely today, because it has been replaced by theories of natural rights that protect negative freedom.

Liberalism in Greece and Rome

In Greece and Rome, the earliest cities developed as centers for independent farmers, artisans and merchants, and some of these cities invented the liberal tradition by developing republican government, civil society, and freedom of thought. As their economies continued to grow, however, inequality increased: Their masses became poorer, while their merchants and aristocratic landowners became wealthy. Despite reforms meant to reduce inequality, Athenian democracy and the Roman republic collapsed after wealth became concentrated, and they ultimately became empires.

The Rise and Fall of Urban Republics

The story of Greece emerges from myth into history at a time when cities were instituting drastic political reforms because they were shocked by worsening economic inequality among citizens. As we will see, Lycurgus's constitution tried to control inequality in a way that made Sparta into a barracks society, while Solon's constitution tried to control inequality in a way that made Athens into the first society with some liberal ideals.

Greece was different from the great civilizations of Egypt, Mesopotamia, India, and China, which were located in river valleys and needed a strong central government to build and manage irrigation projects. In Egypt, for example, the measurement of the Nile floods and management of the irrigation canals were the responsibility of the central government from earliest times. Likewise, the first dynasty of China, the Hsia dynasty, traced its lineage to the legendary sage-king Yu, who organized China to build dams and dykes to tame its floods. In these river-valley societies, monarchs had to be firmly in control to manage irrigation: They were able to burden urban merchants and artisans with such harsh taxes[7] that they never became wealthy enough to challenge the old monarchical form of power based on control of land.

In Greece, centralized government was not necessary to manage irrigation, and the mountainous terrain made communication difficult. Early Greek society was made up of petty kingdoms, and when market towns developed, these local kings were not powerful enough to dominate the towns' craftsmen and merchants completely, as the emperors of the river valley civilizations did.

Cities developed in Greece as centers of trade among economically independent landowners, craftsmen and merchants. Peasants became free-holding landowners who sold food in the market towns and cities. Though the aristocrats who owned large tracts of land remained the most powerful class, they did not completely dominate merchants, artisans, and small farmers. We can get a glimpse of this society in Hesiod's *Works and Days*, written (probably toward the end of the 8th century BC) by a small farmer who believed that hard work, prudence, self-denial, and saving could make him rich.[8]

The earliest urban economies created a society of people who ran their own businesses and who considered themselves citizens, deserving a voice in running their cities. Yet these urban economies also created a new source of inequality: As trade increased, merchants and aristocrats who owned enough land to grow crops for export became increasingly wealthy, while artisans and small landowners became their debtors. This growing inequality led to the constitutional reforms of Lycurgus and Solon.

When Lycurgus created the constitution of Sparta (Plutarch tells us),[9] he confiscated all land and divided it equally among the citizens, giving everyone a plot large enough to produce subsistence but not a surplus. Because the people would not also let him take their personal property and divide it, as he had divided the land, Lycurgus outlawed the use of gold and silver as money and ordered the Spartans to use only iron money, which was so heavy that merchants would not accept it; trade and manufacturing virtually disappeared from Sparta, as Lycurgus had intended. In addition, to eliminate private luxury, Lycurgus turned Sparta into a society where there was virtually no private life: Citizens ate their meals communally, children were taken from their parents at age seven and raised by the polis, and all the citizens were trained as a military machine so they could keep the helots enslaved, to work the land for them. Foreigners were kept out of Sparta, so that they would not spread new ideas. These drastic reforms succeeded in reducing inequality among Spartan citizens temporarily,[10] but they did it by creating a closed society.

Solon's reform of the constitution of Athens was also a reaction against inequality, but it was less drastic than Sparta's. A revolution seemed imminent because growing trade had enriched some Athenians, while many had gone into debt, mortgaged their farms, and faced ruin. Solon's reforms forgave all existing debts and ended imprisonment for debt. His new constitution increased the power of the masses by creating the *Ecclesia* (Assembly) of all citizens, which had to approve any new laws. In a compromise among classes, Solon's constitution limited the Assembly's power; it could only act on business brought before it by the Council of Four Hundred, elected by the four tribes, which were traditionally led by the aristocracy. His constitution also left supreme authority in the hands of the Senate of the Aeropagus, which traditionally represented the aristocracy, but he opened it to all men of wealth. Balancing these concessions to the wealthy, Solon gave the Assembly of all citizens the power to elect the Archons (the military commander and the chief lawmakers), who had previously been chosen by the aristocratic Aeropagus. His constitution also provided that the jurors in the courts should be chosen by lot from all citizens – and it was sometimes said that Solon deliberately made the laws obscure so that the courts could interpret them to the advantage of the common people.

Other reformers who followed Solon continued the redistribution of wealth and power. Pisistratus, a tyrant with popular support, redistributed land that belonged to the city and to banished aristocrats, giving it to the poor. After Pisistratus' death, Cleisthenes modified Solon's constitution and moved it much closer to the classical constitution of Periclean Athens. A new popular Council decided which business to bring before the Assembly, instead of the aristocratic Council of Four Hundred, and the Council also took over most of the powers of the Aeropagus. The members of this council – the most important body in the Athenian government – were not elected but were chosen by lot from all the citizens.

In some ways, classical Athens was far from democratic: Fewer than half the residents were citizens – we can calculate that there were roughly 160,000 citizens, 96,000 *metics* (resident aliens) and 100,000 slaves[11] – and even among citizens, women were barred from public life. In some ways, though, Athens was far more democratic than any government that exists today: It was a direct democracy, where all male citizens could speak to and vote in the assembly that made the laws, and where the Council was chosen by lot from among all the male citizens.

Unlike the reforms in Sparta, the reforms in Athens did not eliminate private life or voluntary associations that were independent of the government. No doubt, Athens' endless political debates helped to stimulate freedom of thought; at the time of Pericles, scientists like Anaxagoras challenged the traditional religious view of nature, and the

Sophists challenged traditional morality. Democratic government, private life separate from the government, and free thought and debate made Athens the earliest society with liberal ideals.

Yet trade continued to increase inequality and class conflict in Athens, despite the repeated redistributions of wealth. Class conflict was submerged temporarily during the golden age, because Athens was so prosperous after it won the Persian War that Pericles was able to pay citizens generously for their jury duty and to build public works projects to provide jobs for the unemployed. But after Athens lost the Peloponnesian War, there was economic decline and bitter hostility between the classes. Athens was governed briefly by a tyranny of thirty aristocrats, which claimed the right to summarily execute anyone not on its list of 3,000 Athenians who remained citizens.[12] Then a popular army drove out the thirty, and established a radically democratic government that executed many aristocrats and their associates – including Socrates.

Through it all, the aristocrats, who were the big land owners, remained the wealthiest and most powerful class. Then, when Alexander the Great conquered Greece and much of Asia, he annexed the old river valley empires. Greek civilization became economically dependent on these agricultural lands, which were far more opulent than Greece itself. The most important center of Hellenistic culture was Alexandria, a harbor that connected the agricultural wealth of the Nile River valley with the other nations around the Mediterranean.

We can see that, as trade increased, Athenian democracy was wracked by increasing inequality, which led to conflict between the masses and the aristocrats who owned most of the land. Ultimately, Athenian democracy was displaced by empires that conquered the old river valley civilizations and controlled their land.

The story of Rome is similar to the story of Greece, though democratic reforms did not go nearly as far in Rome as in Athens. By the fifth century BC, inequality had become so bad that many Roman plebeians were losing their land because of their debts to the patricians, as the Athenians had been in Solon's time. The plebeians mutinied and forced the patrician Senate to create the Tribunes, representatives of the people who could veto the Senate's laws. Inequality continued to increase, and plebeian revolts brought the reforms of the fourth century, which relieved debtors and established the classic Roman constitution, where the Senate was joined by a second legislative body, the Tribal Assembly, where plebeians had almost as much representation as patricians.

Despite these reforms, the plebeians became more impoverished as trade grew. After Rome conquered territory around the Mediterranean and imported slaves to work large plantations in Italy and Sicily, small farmers could not support themselves by working their land, so they were forced to move from the countryside to the city of Rome. The Roman republic ended when these urban masses supported Caesar, who promised them a share of the spoils of empire. Order was restored when Augustus made himself Emperor and began providing bread and circuses for the urban masses – bread made of grain grown in the river valley of Egypt, which Augustus had conquered.

In Rome as in Greece, land remained the main source of wealth. Under the Roman Republic, as trade increased, there were constant conflicts between the impoverished plebeians and the wealthy patricians who owned most of the land. Finally, the Roman republic was replaced by an empire based on the wealth of the river valley lands.

When the capitol of the Roman Empire moved to Constantinople, it was moving to a more central location, between Rome and the older river-valley civilizations that were the economic base of the Roman empire. During Europe's dark ages, the great river valleys remained centers of civilization governed by various empires.

Forerunners of Liberal Thought

The Greeks never developed a full-blown liberal political theory, because liberal ideals collapsed before political philosophy flourished. The popular democracy that drove out the thirty after the Peloponnesian war rejected key liberal ideals, such as free speech. Under Pericles, Anaxagoras was free to claim that the sun was a ball of fire rather than a god, but under this democracy, Socrates was charged with denying that the sun was a god when he was tried and executed for corrupting the youth of Athens by making them think critically about the city's traditions. This government discredited democracy before the Greeks wrote any major political philosophy. Alexander's conquests ended Greek democracy and political philosophy not long afterwards.

One hint that we have of classical Athens' political ideals is the famous funeral oration of Pericles, reported by Thucidides:

> Our constitution is called a democracy because power is in the hands not of a minority but of the whole people. When it is a question of settling private disputes, everyone is equal before the law; when it is a question of putting one person before another in a position of public responsibility, what

counts is not membership of a particular class, but the actual ability which the man possesses. No one, so long as he has it in him to be of service to the state, is kept in political obscurity because of poverty. And, just as our political life is free and open, so is our day to day life in our relations with each other.... We are free and tolerant in our private lives; but in our public affairs, we keep to the law.[13]

This is quoted from a speech that a politician delivered on a formal occasion, so we can assume that it is a fairly conventional statement of classical Athenian political ideals, and it is filled with ideas that we would call liberal. It not only talks about democracy, equal opportunity and the rule of law, but it also emphasizes that Athenians – in an obvious contrast with the Spartans – have private lives that are not controlled by the government.

Yet the first major book of Athenian political philosophy, written a generation later, was Plato's *Republic*, which rejects democracy and calls for a totalitarian state where there is no private life. Plato was an aristocrat – a cousin of Critias, the leader of the thirty aristocrats who governed Athens after the Peloponnesian War – and he was disgusted by the excesses of the Athenian democracy that drove out the thirty and executed Socrates.

Reacting against Plato, Aristotle wrote the first book of political philosophy that includes some basic liberal principles, his *Politics*. He criticized Plato's totalitarian republic by calling for a pluralistic society.[14] He took it for granted that, in a free society, people would manage their own households and form voluntary associations that were independent of the government.[15] He considered inequality a danger to democracy and believed that a middle class government is most stable.¹⁶ To prevent self-government from becoming a tyranny of the majority, he called for a government of laws, not of men, with a division of power between the executive, judicial and deliberative branches of government.¹⁷ He was the first to talk about division of powers among the branches of government, so they would check and balance each other and none would have excessive power – an idea that would become central to the American constitution.

Yet Aristotle was essentially conservative. Like Plato, he was disgusted by the excesses of democracy after the Peloponnesian War, and he wanted to protect traditional liberties but did not want democracy to go too far. In his experience, the main threat to the rule of law was the *demos*, the masses who were poor and who could expropriate the property of the rich if they controlled the government. He expected democracies to serve the self-interest of the masses, and so he believed that the most important check and balance within government was a two-house legislature, with the upper house representing the wealthy and the lower house representing all the citizens.¹⁸ Aristotle called his preferred form of government a "polity," which means a constitutional or lawful government, and he thought that balancing the two classes would prevent the masses from overriding the law, as they tended to do in a democracy. Because Aristotle described it as a combination of democracy and oligarchy, the polity was also called a "mixed system" of government.

As a conservative, Aristotle also believed that only wealthy male landowners were fully capable of freedom. At the very beginning of *Politics*, as a fundamental principle of government, he says that women and slaves are naturally inferior to freemen.¹⁹ He believed that laborers and slaves must work to make freedom possible for a small class of property owners (unless, he says in one passage, the old myth came true and machines began to move themselves, so masters had no need for slaves).[20] In addition to the "mixed system," which he thought was the best government that was practical for existing Greek cities, Aristotle described an ideal government where all of the citizens were wealthy slave owners.[21]

After Aristotle, and after the conquests of Alexander, political philosophy almost disappeared in Greece. The most important schools of philosophy were Epicureanism and stoicism, which both searched for a way to find peace of mind in one's personal life, at a time when there was no longer democratic political life.

The stoics believed (like Socrates) that we could know by reason what actions are good and bad. And they believed that, because the capacity for moral reasoning is part of human nature, all people are equal – even women and non-Greeks – in the sense that all are capable of understanding the natural law and of making moral judgments for themselves.[22] The emphasis on equality and the natural right to make moral judgments for yourself seems liberal, but the stoics were only thinking of a sort of inner equality and autonomy, not of political changes that would give everyone freedom in practice. They believed that you could live virtuously no matter what your external situation, and they said that people should accept whatever government exists. They had no motive to move beyond moral philosophy to political philosophy,[23] because the rise of empires had made political philosophy unimportant.

There was no more reason for liberal political philosophy to be written in Rome than there had been in Greece. Cicero was the first to write philosophy in Latin, and he wrote just as the Roman republic was collapsing, long after the plebeians had become an urban mob. In his moral and political philosophy, he combined the stoics' idea that everyone is capable of moral autonomy with Aristotle's emphasis on republican politics, which came naturally to him as Roman Senator:

> we are designed by nature for activity. ...the most important [activities] are, first, ... study of ... nature ...; secondly, the practice and theory of politics; thirdly, the principles of ... the ... virtues and the activities consonant therewith.[24]

This idea that moral and political autonomy are central to human nature could have been the basis of a genuinely liberal political philosophy, if only Cicero had taken it seriously enough.

Cicero did affirm many essential principles of liberalism, which were present in the Roman republic. For example, he said that laws should be general decrees binding on all rather than "laws of personal exception" that apply to individuals,[25] which is another way of saying that there should be a government of laws, not of men. He said that legislatures should act on one question at a time and give both magistrates and private citizens the opportunity to speak on each question,[26] guaranteeing freedom of speech for the public. He said that a constitution must define the responsibilities of public officials clearly and let officials act only in their own capacity,[27] and that it should balance the interests of different groups to prevent any one from acting tyrannically – the ideas of division of powers and checks and balances, which he (like Aristotle) believed were needed to protect the hereditary aristocracy from the impoverished masses.

Yet Cicero was less a philosopher than he was a lawyer, pleading the case of the Roman plutocracy that he belonged to. There are times when he is obviously trying to justify the privileges of the upper classes, rather than thinking critically about what is a good society and a good constitution. For example, he says that he is against the secret ballot because it has "deprived the aristocracy of all its influence"[28] by making it harder to buy votes. Instead, he recommends oral voting because it "grants the appearance of liberty [and] preserves the influence of the aristocracy ...."[29] These are not the words of someone whose goal is to create a just society based on natural law.

The Roman republic collapsed during his time, and there were no philosophers after Cicero who carried these political ideas to their logical conclusion. A liberal political philosopher would not have lived long under the emperors.

Though no single philosopher formulated them, most of the fundamental principles of liberalism were present in inchoate form in ancient times. All citizens should be involved in governing the state. In addition to the state, there should be an independent civil society made up of families and voluntary associations. The legislature should pass laws that apply equally to everyone. Citizens should have the right to speak about these laws before they are passed. A constitution should include a division of power with checks and balances, so it does not become a tyranny of the majority.

It is tempting to believe that, if only Athenian democracy or the Roman republic had lasted long enough, some philosopher would have risen above class interest and woven these ideas into the first liberal political theory. In reality, only wealthy males were free, but a philosopher might have imagined a society where everyone was free – rather than just saying that everyone has inner freedom, as the stoics did. Aristotle hints at this theory on the rare occasions when he says it is possible to have a democracy ruled by law[30] and adds that (though he disagrees) many of his contemporaries believe there is most freedom in a democracy where all people have an equal say in the government.[31] Perhaps one of those contemporaries did write a book of liberal political philosophy that did not survive.

Liberalism in the Middle Ages and After

The story of modern Europe begins like the story of ancient Greece and Rome. Medieval cities began as independent centers of artisans and merchants, where free institutions developed (though landowners kept power in the countryside). But the rise of trade enriched merchants and landowners, undermining these free institutions. The free cities of the middle ages were swallowed up by absolute rulers who became powerful by building empires in the new world, much as the free cities of ancient times were swallowed up by absolute rulers who became powerful by building empires in the old river valleys.

In modern times, though, urban economies were becoming so important that they could not be completely overshadowed by the wealth of the empires' land, as they had been in ancient Greece and Rome. Urban economies were beginning to produce more wealth than the agricultural economies that surrounded them. As long as land ownership remained more important economically, classical liberalism was distorted by older aristocratic ideals, as it had been in ancient times; ultimately, as industry become more important economically, liberalism was distorted by new commercial ideals.

The Rise of the Medieval City

Like ancient cities, medieval cities began as centers of trade and handicraft production, but they developed more independently of landed interests than cities had in classical times. The aristocracy generally kept out of urban politics, except in Italy, and slavery was not central to the economies of medieval cities, as it had been to ancient cities. Though there were some slaves, it is significant that living in a city for a year and a day freed serfs from feudal obligations: As the medieval adage said, "City air makes free."

Labor-saving technology developed more quickly in medieval cities than in ancient cities, which relied on slaves to do the hard labor. For example, the Domesday Book says that there were already 5000 water mills in England in 1086, and within a century, mills were using gear systems to power fast-moving machinery – for example, in saw mills.

In a first step in self-government, the merchants and craftsmen of each city formed guilds to regulate their occupations. In part, the guilds were associations for mutual aid: Members helped each other in illness, joined in holidays and religious ceremonies, and paved the streets of their towns. In part, they were an attempt to limit competition and maintain prices: Guilds persuaded towns to keep out goods that competed with their own, they set a "just price" for goods, and they tried to stop the sale of inferior goods – often by putting their "hallmark" (the mark of the Guild Hall) on quality products. The guilds in each city could control trade in this way, because most goods were produced for local use.

Only master craftsmen and independent merchants could join these guilds, but after a long apprenticeship and two or three years as a journeyman (a day laborer, from the

French *journee*), any workman could set himself up as master of his own establishment, if he could save enough capital and pass the guild's test of his competence. The legend of Dick Whittington, the poor boy who became Lord Mayor of London,[32] shows how different medieval cities were from the surrounding feudal society, where rank was hereditary, and from ancient cities, where the old aristocracy remained preeminent.

Economic independence spread from the cities to the countryside. Aristocrats wanted cash from the peasants, rather than payment in kind, so they could buy the luxury products for sale in the cities. Serfs were able to earn cash, because the cities needed to buy food – and they could also gain their freedom by escaping to the cities, which needed labor.[33] To keep their peasants, land owners sold freedom to serfs who could afford it, and then leased land to these free peasants. Gradually in western Europe, from the twelfth through the sixteenth century, serfdom was replaced by peasant ownership.

Sometimes, cities fought for the right to self-government, but more often their growing wealth and influence won them this freedom. In England, William the Conqueror gave London a charter of self-government in order to win the city's support against the nobility, and Henry II gave many cities charters for the same reason. Many other English cities bought their freedom from Richard I, who needed money to prepare for his crusade, and Cambridge bought its freedom from King John, who needed money to pay his debts. In Spain, kings also gave royal charters to many cities in order to win their support against the nobility – beginning with Leon, which received its charter from the King of Castile in 1020. In the low countries, lords often gave charters of partial freedom to cities to encourage commercial development, which generated revenue for them. In France, cities were more likely to fight violently for their freedom: Some never succeeded, but most cities of Northern France gained their freedom between 1080 and 1200 – and went on to build the Gothic cathedrals. In German speaking countries, the central government was even weaker than in the rest of Europe, and cities had more independence: The first moves toward German unification began when free cities formed leagues to promote trade, such as the Rhenish league and the Hanseatic League.

In a few places, popular interests rose up and freed their countries entirely from feudal authorities. In Switzerland, a mountainous country that was hard to control militarily, three cantons defeated the Hapsburgs in 1315, and ten cantons had freed themselves completely of feudal obligations by 1499. The Netherlands, whose location at the mouth of the Rhine made it a center of trade, rebelled against the Spanish Hapsburgs in 1566, and drove the Spanish troops from seven provinces by 1600.

In most of Europe, popular government was limited to the cities, while the king and aristocracy continued to rule the countryside and to control national affairs. Urban interests were represented in the English Parliament, the French Estates General, the German Diet and the Spanish Cortes, but they were a minority and had little influence on the national government. At the same time, the king and nobility looked down on the bourgeoisie and did not bother with urban government. Italy was the exception, the only country where aristocrats took an active part in city government: The aristocratic Ghibelline party, which supported the Emperor, struggled against the bourgeois Guelf party, which supported the Pope because it was afraid a strong Emperor would undermine the cities' freedoms.

These medieval communes were far from being perfect democracies. Usually, only guild masters had the vote, and the wealthier merchant guilds tried from the beginning to get more power than the crafts guilds. Yet these medieval communes were an important step toward popular government, and they are the source of our own democratic traditions. The English are wrong to trace their freedom to the Barons who made King John sign the Magna Carta; the French revolutionaries had a better grasp of history when they deposed the king and named their democratic government the Paris commune.

The commune of Florence, which produced important republican political theorists, is a good example of how the guilds moved toward a limited form of democratic government. The merchant and crafts guilds worked together to disenfranchise the nobility in 1282, and then they immediately began to fight against each other for power. After suppressing the revolution of 1378, when small craftsmen and workers took control of the city government and declared a moratorium on debts, Florence developed its classical constitution, which recognized two groups of guilds: The *arti maggiori* (major guilds) included merchants, financiers, manufacturers and others, who were known as the *popolo grasso* (the fat people), and the *arti minori* (minor guilds) included butchers, bakers, cobblers, carpenters, innkeepers and others, who were known as the *popolo minuto* (the little people). Every voter had to be a member of one of these guilds: Laborers did not have the vote, and aristocrats had to join guilds to vote. The upper house of the legislature and the eight priors, who chose the head of state, were both divided equally between the major and the minor guilds. The lower house represented all the voters equally, so it was dominated by the minor guilds, but it was only allowed to act on measures placed before it by the priors. During crises, the priors could call a *parlimento* of all voters to assemble in the Piazza del Signoria and choose a reform commission that would have supreme power for a limited time.

The representative governments of medieval cities stand in sharp contrast to the authoritarian monarchy, nobility, and church of the time. The bourgeoisie was inventing liberal institutions in Italian cities, and it had even more influence in other parts of Europe, where the aristocracy kept away from city government entirely.

The Rise of Empires

According to popular history, absolute monarchs and aristocrats controlled Europe during the middle ages and Renaissance, and the movement toward democracy did not begin until the seventeenth and eighteenth century. In reality, the movement toward democracy began in the medieval cities, and absolute monarchy emerged later, during the Renaissance, as kings gained immense wealth and power by conquering land in the new world. Republican urban governments lost their power to empires in Europe during the Renaissance, much as they had in ancient times.

The changing fortunes of the Spanish monarchy provide the most dramatic example. Charles V was a very powerful medieval monarch, the head of an empire that stretched from Italy to the Netherlands as well as to the new world, and he met resistance from the popular governments of the time. In Spain, he was the head of four kingdoms, Navarre, Valencia, Aragon-Castille, and Catalonia, each with its own assembly. When he was crowned in Aragon, the assembly declared that it was a republic and he was an elective king who would keep their allegiance only as long as he obeyed their laws. His wars to dominate Europe left him insolvent, so he abdicated, leaving his territories in central Europe to his brother Ferdinand and Spain and the empire in the new world to his son Philip. Then, in 1545, silver was discovered in Peru, and the crown's revenue from this source became the basis of royal absolutism in Spain.[34]

Likewise, in France, the Estates General virtually stopped meeting after the monarchy became wealthy under Henry IV. The French monarchs had new sources of revenue and no longer needed to convene this assembly to levy new taxes.

We can see how the mercantile economy, empires, and royal absolutism replaced the older urban governments of Europe by looking at how the different characters of today's European countries grew out of this transition.

In Switzerland, the land-locked, mountainous terrain discouraged mercantilism and made self-defense easy. As late as the nineteenth century, its economy was still based on small independent farms and on crafts such as watch making, and the free institutions of the middle ages remained strong. Today, Switzerland remains the least progressive of the west European countries in some ways, because it was not transformed by commercial values as rapidly as the nations around it: For example, women did not get the vote until 1971, and it steadfastly refuses to join the European Union, which its neighbors consider the wave of the future. But in many ways, it remains the most democratic of the west European countries, because it preserved the spirit of its old medieval institutions: It is the only one that has direct democracy, where citizen initiatives can pass new laws and overturn laws passed by the national government.

In most of Europe, by contrast, trade increased rapidly during the middle ages and the Renaissance, bringing inequality that undermined the free institutions of medieval cities.

In Florence, the popular republic established during the middle ages ended when the wealthiest family of bankers, the Medici, became powerful enough to set themselves up as rulers. In 1434, Cosimo de' Medici made his family the effective rulers of Florence, retaining the old republican forms but using his wealth to manipulate and control politics from behind the scenes,[35] and the Medici established themselves formally as a hereditary dynasty in 1537. But Italy's cities could not defend themselves from invasions by the increasingly powerful monarchs around them: For example, the French invaded Italy in 1494, causing the Medici to lose power until the Spanish restored them in 1512. Though it was the glory of Europe during the Renaissance, Italy ultimately became one of the weaker countries in western Europe, because it did not have a strong monarchy to impose a central government and to conquer an empire.

In Spain, Portugal, France, and Britain – on the western rim of Europe, closest to America – the monarchy and aristocracy became powerful during the Renaissance, because the discovery of the new world let them build vast empires, which were ruled by their monarchs, which were dominated by their wealthy merchants and aristocrats, and which were worked by slave labor.

With the rise of absolutism and empire, Spain, Portugal, France, and Britain seemed to be going the way of ancient Greece and Rome, whose urban republics were replaced by empires based on conquered lands. But Europe's commercial economy had already developed to the point where this could not happen. For a country to thrive, it needed a monarch powerful enough to conquer an empire, but it also needed a commercial class energetic enough to exploit this empire.

Spain and Portugal had powerful monarchs, who controlled the greatest empires of the Renaissance, but they did not have strong commercial classes. As a result, these nations stagnated economically, despite all the wealth they extracted from their empires' plantations and mines, and they remained economically backward until recently. Their decline was a sign that manufacturing and commerce had become a more important source of wealth than land.

The low countries were filled with wealthy merchants and manufacturers but did not have a strong monarch. Flanders had Europe's most advanced manufacturing economy during the middle ages, and the Netherlands had Europe's most advanced commercial economy in the 17th century. But Flanders never developed a central government, and it lost its independence. The Dutch Republic had the smallest of the Renaissance empires, and it lost New Amsterdam to Britain in 1667. Because they did not have strong monarchs, the low countries, which had been Europe's economic leaders, became backwaters: By the nineteenth century, they were known primarily for their quaint architecture and their picturesque old windmills.

France had both a strong monarch and energetic merchants, and they worked together during the 17th century, when Jean Baptiste Colbert was Louis XIV's trade minister. The son of a cloth merchant, Colbert decided to develop the nation's economy by promoting luxury exports in the aristocratic French style, saying "With our taste let us make war on Europe, and through fashion conquer the world."[36] Because the landed and merchant classes worked together in this way, Louis XIV was Europe's most powerful absolute monarch, and Paris was Europe's most magnificent capital. France has remained a center of style and culture ever since.

In Britain, the alliance between landowners and merchants increased the power of the monarchy during the Renaissance, but the political winds shifted back and forth suddenly during the seventeenth century.

Because the landed and merchant classes worked together under their rule, Henry VIII and Elizabeth I became powerful and magnificent Renaissance monarchs, in the style of France's Louis XIV. Under Henry VIII, the English monarchy and aristocracy enriched themselves by enclosing land that had been commons and using it to produce wool, which was exported to the low countries and used to manufacture textiles for the world market. Under Queen Elizabeth, aristocrats colonized the new world and helped create trade in agricultural goods – most famously when aristocrats such as Sir Walter Raleigh helped create the trade in tobacco.

But after Elizabeth's death, the Stuart kings refused to work with commercial interests. James I made a treaty in 1604 that let the Spanish dominate trade with America, in an attempt to strengthen himself and weaken the commercial interests in Parliament. His famous campaign against the immorality of smoking tobacco was meant to accommodate Spain by discouraging English trade with the new world. He executed Sir Walter Raleigh in 1618, after Raleigh's men destroyed a Spanish settlement while searching for gold in Guiana – making Raleigh a hero of the commercial and Puritan party. Like James I, Charles I refused to work with commercial interests: For example, he advised English merchants to stay out of the Mediterranean, rather than providing naval protection for them, and the Grand Remonstrance of 1641 complained that thousands of English seamen had been enslaved by the Turks because of Charles' negligence.37

Because the Stuarts were undermining commerce, England's wealthy merchants united with its smallholders against the monarchy during the early seventeenth century, and the Puritan rebellion executed Charles I and declared England a Commonwealth in 1649. However, the Commonwealth lasted only ten years. In 1660, the Restoration ended the influence of the smallholders permanently, and in 1688, the Glorious Revolution put English government securely in the hands of wealthy commercial interests, who gave Britain the world's richest economy and largest empire.

Because of the political chaos in England, there was an outpouring of political philosophy during these decades. Classical liberal thinkers such as James Harrington became influential during the Puritan rebellion, Hobbes' defense of absolute monarchy became influential during the restoration, and Locke's new commercial version of liberalism became influential after the Glorious Revolution. Variations on commercial liberalism have been central to English political philosophy ever since.

Classical Liberal Thought

During the early middle ages, Christians believed in inner freedom, as the stoics had. Man or women, free or slave, Jew or and Greek, all were equally free to accept salvation – but this spiritual equality had nothing to do with worldly affairs. Saint Augustine attacked Cicero for arguing that there could be a good society in this world, corrupted by original sin. He believed that government must restrain our sinful natures and enforce the peace, that even unjust governments could do this, and that Christians should not care about their place in the worldly order: "rich, poor, free, slave, male, or female, they are bound to tolerate even the worst, and if need be, the most atrocious form of government."[38]

Our liberal tradition grew from two strands of thinking that appeared during the late middle ages and Renaissance. The civic humanists in Florence developed republican political theory. Radical Protestants focused on freedom of conscience. Both these strands influenced James Harrington, the most important political theorist during England's Puritan rebellion. Thus, both influenced the American revolutionaries, as James Harrington was an important source of the Jeffersonian ideal of a republic of small farmers and businessmen.

The Civic Republicans

The earliest of the Florentine civic republicans, Leonardo Bruni, is one of the few forerunners of liberalism who wrote before the free government of his city collapsed: He had been writing for thirty years before Cosimo de' Medici established his family as rulers of Florence in 1434. In his description of the commune of Florence, which he modeled on Pericles' funeral oration, Bruni wrote that people develop virtue by participating in the political life of their city, choosing its magistrates, and making its laws, and he claimed that civic virtue is common in Florence, because most of its offices are open to all its citizens. He argued that virtue, arts and letters thrive in free, open societies and decay under empires.[39]

The more important Florentine civic republicans – Guicciardini, Giannotti and Machiavelli – wrote after the fall of the popular government, when there was a power struggle between the Medici and Florence's wealthy citizens, called the *ottimati*.

These thinkers extended the earlier republican ideal in some ways. Guicciardini formulated the republican definition of freedom, which is shared by political theorists who are reviving civic republican ideas in American today: Freedom means that you are bound by laws that you have a voice in making. This implies both that there is citizen self-government and that there is a rule of law rather than of men.[40]

To give the wealthy *ottimati* more power, however, the civic republicans also revived Aristotle's ideal of a "mixed system" of government, with elements of aristocracy and democracy. Giannotti used Venice's government as an example of a mixed system. When Medici power collapsed, from 1494 to 1512 and from 1527 to 1530, the Florentine republic adopted a constitution modeled on Venice's, though the people had more influence than the Civic Republicans had expected. Both Florence and Venice were actually commercial republics, with the bankers and merchants vying for power,[41] but the civic humanists used Aristotle's old aristocratic model of a mixed system to describe them.

The civic humanists also ignored classical natural law theory. Machiavelli was notorious for believing that there was no higher reason than reason of state: The prince could do whatever was necessary to keep power and was not obligated to a higher moral law. Within a republic, there was no higher law than the laws passed by the citizens. Virtue was nothing more than civic virtue.

Freedom of Conscience

Civic republicanism became important to contemporary American legal and political philosophy several decades ago, after J.G.A. Pocock showed that these Florentine thinkers influenced James Harrington and Thomas Jefferson,[42] but Pocock and the civic republicans did not see that Christian natural law theory is equally important to our liberal tradition.

In some ways, Thomas Aquinas was more liberal than the civic humanists. He wrote that Christians have the duty to disobey unjust laws and that a community has a right to depose its king if he rules unjustly[43] – ideas that led Lord Acton to say that Aquinas produced "the earliest exposition of the Whig theory of the revolution."[44] Both of these ideas became the conventional wisdom of late medieval political philosophy, but they would not have made any sense to Machiavelli and the civic humanists, who believed there was no higher standard of justice than the law of the state.

Thomas Aquinas meant his theory to give the church more power over temporal rulers: The church would decide which kings and which laws are unjust. The Protestant reformers went much further by saying that Christians must also depose the church's hierarchy and disobey its laws if the church becomes corrupt.

Freedom of conscience was the key principle struggling to emerge during the Protestant Reformation. It was behind the debates over the meaning of communion, for example: Catholics claimed that salvation was impossible without sacraments, so anyone the church excommunicated went to hell, but most Protestants believed that salvation depended not on external rituals but on one's own sincere inward turning to God, so the church hierarchy could not condemn you to eternal torment by excommunicating you. Likewise, Catholics did not encourage Bible reading and expected believers to accept the Church's teachings, but Protestants were encouraged to read the Bible and think about its meaning for themselves.

Radical Protestant sects carried freedom of conscience furthest, saying that acts have no religious value unless they are done freely. The Anabaptists in continental Europe and the Baptists in England rejected infant baptism because they believed that the ritual of baptism was worthless unless you freely decided to enter into it as an adult. The Quakers rejected all ritual: At their meetings, the group sits silently waiting until one of them feels moved to speak according to the prompting of the inner light. Because they believed that anyone can be moved by the inner light, Quakers let women preach, and many opposed slavery.

The American colonies that were founded by radical Protestants were the first places in the world that allowed freedom of religion. In 1636, Rhode Island was founded by the Baptist Roger Williams, a firm believer of freedom of conscience, and it immediately became a haven for Anabaptists, Quakers and others persecuted for their religious beliefs. In 1682, Pennsylvania was founded by the Quaker William Penn, whose written Frame of Government guaranteed freedom of religion. This is the one basic liberal principle that is missing in the Greek and Roman philosophers, who take it for granted that people will go along with established religious rituals, even if they are skeptical about them, and that is also missing from the civic republicans.

James Harrington

James Harrington, the most important liberal political philosopher writing during England's Puritan rebellion, was influenced by the civic republicans, but he was also influenced by radical Protestantism. He believed in congregational self-government,⁴⁵ and he said that freedom of religion and civil liberty were both essential to a democracy:

> Democracy, being nothing but entire liberty, and liberty of conscience without civil liberty or civil liberty without liberty of conscience being but liberty by halves, must admit liberty of conscience....⁴⁶

He also used Christian natural law philosophy to argue for popular government because it is most likely to make decisions that conform to right reason – quoting from Richard Hooker, England's most important natural law philosopher.⁴⁷ These ideas are alien to the Florentine civic humanists, whose highest ideal was the citizen's loyalty to the republic and its laws.

Harrington borrowed the "mixed system" of government from Aristotle and the civic humanists. In his version, the upper house initiates laws and the lower house passes or rejects them, and there must be a strict division of power between these legislative bodies and the magistracy (his term for both the executive and judiciary) that executes the laws.⁴⁸ He insisted that the chief executive should be answerable to the people, who must have the right to remove him if he acts outside the law:⁴⁹ Aristotle wanted to restrain the people, but Harrington, writing in Cromwell's England, believed it was more important to restrain the chief executive if you wanted to preserve a government of laws rather then of men.

Harrington wrote that freedom depends on ownership of productive property.⁵⁰ In his ideal republic, citizens would work their own land: Most farms would be large enough that people could support themselves in "convenient plenty" but small enough "to keep the plough in the hand of the owners, and not mere hirelings."⁵¹ To prevent wealth and power from becoming too concentrated, he supported an "agrarian law" requiring large land owners to divide their property among their heirs when they died.[52]

Harrington was writing under Cromwell's Commonwealth, and some of his ideas look as if they were intended to heal the divisions of the time. He argued for an established church, for example, by saying that people should all have freedom of conscience to worship as they choose, but the majority should also have the freedom to follow its conscience and establish a national church[53] – and here he seems to be trying to find a compromise that would please everyone. He also argued that a country is better for having a hereditary aristocracy.[54] He expected his agrarian law would leave England with an aristocracy of 5000 wealthy, landed families, who would be protected by the upper house of the legislature, but that it would stop excessive concentration of wealth and power; he did not realize that the real threat came from England's commercial interests, which were becoming wealthier than its landed interests.[55]

Despite his compromises, Harrington is the writer who came closest to stating the classical liberal ideal. He believed in republican self-government with division of powers and checks and balances to prevent the tyranny of the majority. He believed in preserving private life separate from the government, as people run their own farms, businesses and independent churches. And he believed in freedom of conscience.

Just as important, he wanted a society where small proprietors manage their own farms, where congregants manage their own churches, and where there are term limits on government offices, so every citizen has an opportunity to be part of the government.⁵⁶ In other words, he believed in positive freedom.

Harrington is no longer well known – probably because his prose is so hard to read – but at the time of the American revolution his name was a household word.⁵⁷ Harrington was an important influence on the American tradition of civil liberty, freedom of conscience, and checks and balances: The president of Yale college said in a sermon of 1783 that the highest praise he could give to the governments of the New England states was that they had "realized the capital ideas of Harrington's *Oceana*."⁵⁸ And Harrington's idea that a republic should be made up primarily of farmers who work their own land inspired the Jeffersonians in early America.

Moral Individualism

Classical liberalism developed a theory of natural rights that was based on natural law: We have a right to make decisions for ourselves, because we all have a moral faculty that lets us understand what is right and wrong.

This classical theory of natural rights is the ancestor of the idea of civil disobedience, which is an important part of America's liberal tradition. For example, it was a key tactic of the civil rights movement of the mid-twentieth century. Civil disobedience is one element of the liberal tradition that is derived solely from the moral individualism of classical liberalism and that could not possibly be a product of the self-interested individualism of laissez-faire liberalism. It is worthwhile to look in detail at the classical theory of natural rights and of civil disobedience, because they show that we cannot fully explain contemporary liberalism if we overlook classical liberalism.

The conflict between authority and conscience, which became the basis of the classical theory of natural rights, is central to Sophocles' play *Antigone*. The play opens after a battle where Antigone's brothers, Etiocles and Polynices, have killed each other. Creon, the tyrant of Thebes, has ordered that Etiocles be buried because he was loyal to Creon, and that Polynices be denied burial because he fought against Creon. Antigone disobeys Creon's orders and buries Polynices, saying that she is obeying a higher law. Throughout the play, Sophocles emphasizes the conflict between natural law and the positive law of the state: For example, Antigone tells Creon that she does not "think your orders were so strong / that you, a mortal man, could overrun / the gods' unwritten and unfailing laws," while Creon says that "The man the state has put in place must have / obedient hearing to his least command / when it is right, and even when it's not." Creon sentences Antigone to be imprisoned permanently in a cave, but when the prophet Tieresias says that his action will lead to disaster, Creon relents and goes to release her, only to find that Antigone has killed herself and that his own son and wife are also dead. When the chorus first hears Creon's orders, at the beginning of the play, they say "you can make such rulings as you will, about the living and about the dead" – repeating the conventional wisdom that the law of the state is supreme – but at the end of the play, Creon admits he was wrong, and the chorus says that he has learned justice too late.[59]

Throughout the play, Creon says repeatedly that he cannot give in to a woman, and the play makes it very clear that his conventional belief in male authority is wrong, because a woman has the same understanding of the moral law and the same obligation to obey the moral law as a man.

In *Antigone,* Sophocles asks whether morality is based on some higher law or is nothing more than a convention imposed by the state. The same question became central to Greek philosophy. The question was forced on the Greeks when trade brought them into contact with other peoples, and they found that the Egyptians, Persians, Mesopotamians, and Phoenicians were more advanced in many ways than they themselves were, but (as we can see in Herodotus) they were struck by how totally different these society's customs were from their own.

The Sophists were moral relativists, who looked at the different customs of the civilizations around them and concluded that moral and political ideals were merely social conventions, with no real validity. Protagoras believed that morality is just a matter of taste: If one man says food tastes good to him and another says the same food tastes bad to him, they are both right, and if one man says an action seems just to him and another says the same action seems unjust to him, they are also both right. Thrasymachus believed (like Marx) that a society's moral system is just an ideology that its rulers use to keep their power; he said that justice was "the will of the strongest." Callicles believed (like Nietzsche) that justice was created by the masses, who are weak and invent morality to control the few who are strong.[60]

Socrates rejected this moral relativism and claimed that – apart from all of the ethical systems of different nations, and apart from the traditions of our own nation – there are moral truths that we can know through reason.[61] It is hard to know what Socrates' own opinions were, because he argued by accepting his opponents' premises and showing that they led to contradictions,[62] but it is clear that he believed reason can find objective moral truth, as he says in Plato's *Gorgias* and *Protagoras,* where he

50

disputes with the two leading sophists.[63] This was Socrates' most important idea, and the major schools of philosophy that followed – the Platonists, Aristotelians, Stoics, and Epicureans – all claimed that they were the successors to Socrates because they all searched for objective moral truth. Stoic philosophers first used the term "natural law" to mean the moral good that we can know by reason, independent of social conventions.

Greek philosophers never developed a liberal theory of natural rights based on natural law, though *Antigone* points toward such a theory, because the popular government that executed Socrates discredited democracy, and Alexander's conquests ended democracy not long afterwards.

Cicero seems to be the first philosopher who hinted at a theory of natural rights by saying that each person can understand the natural law and should follow the natural law even if it conflicts with the state's law:

> True law is right reason in agreement with nature; it is of universal application, unchanging and everlasting ... We cannot be freed from its obligations by senate or people, and we need not look outside ourselves for an expounder or interpreter of it.[64]

Cicero believed that moral autonomy is central to the good life, and this idea could form the basis of a theory of natural rights, but Cicero never developed this theory fully, and there was no chance for political philosophers to develop it under the Roman empire.

Thomas Aquinas and his followers were the first to develop an explicit theory of natural rights. Aquinas believed that people have a right to disobey unjust laws that harm them and have an obligation to disobey unjust laws that are contrary to God's law:

Laws framed by man are either just or unjust. If they be just, they have the power of binding in conscience, from the eternal law whence they are derived .... On the other hand, laws may be unjust in two ways: first, by being contrary to human good ... as when an authority imposes on his subjects burdensome laws, conducive, not to the common good but to his own cupidity or vainglory.... The like are acts of violence rather than laws.... Wherefore such laws do not bind in conscience, except perhaps in order to avoid scandal or disturbance, for which cause a man should even yield his right.... Secondly, laws may be unjust through being opposed to the Divine good: such are the laws of tyrants inducing to idolatry, or to anything else contrary to the Divine law: and laws of this kind must nowise be observed....[65]

Medieval legal theorists accepted Thomas Aquinas' idea that we have a right or an obligation to disobey unjust laws, and they used it as the basis of the first theory that explicitly distinguished natural rights from natural law. The Latin *ius naturalis* can be translated either as natural law or as natural right. Medieval lawyers distinguished between these two meanings by saying that *ius naturalis* can refer both to the *norma agendi*, the law that governs action, and the *facultas agendi*, the right to act, and they held that the right to act follows from the law that governs action:[66] You have a right to act in a way that violates the state's laws when these laws conflict with the higher natural law that should govern your actions.

Though Catholics expected the Church to interpret the natural law, radical Protestants believed in freedom of conscience – in the freedom to make your own decisions about religion and sometimes also in the freedom to make your own moral and political decisions. James Harrington believed that democracy requires both civil liberty and freedom of conscience, and he also expected people to assert their civil liberties when they were obligated to do so by conscience: "Men who have the means to assert liberty of conscience have the means to assert civil liberty, and they will do it if they are oppressed in their consciences."[67]

The greatest writer of the Puritan rebellion, John Milton, also based civil liberties on freedom of conscience. Like other radical Protestants, he believed in freedom of religion because he believed an act has no moral value if it is done under constraint – and he believed in freedom of speech, freedom of the press and the right to divorce for the same reason. For example, he defends freedom of the press in *Areopagitica* by saying:

> If every action which is good, or evil in man at ripe years, were to be under pittance, and prescription, and compulsion, what were vertue but a name, what praise could then be due to well-doing …? many there be that complain of divin Providence for suffering *Adam* to transgresse, foolish tongues! When God gave him reason, he gave him freedom to choose …; he had been else a meer artificiall *Adam*, such an *Adam* as he is in the motions. We ourselves esteem not of that obedience, or love, or gift, which is of force ….[68]

We can see that classical liberalism bases our natural rights on our moral responsibilities. This does not mean, as we sometimes say today, that for every right, there is a corresponding responsibility – for example, that you have a right to drive a car but a responsibility to be careful. It means that the right is almost identical to the responsibility. You have a right to speak up about political issues, because you have an obligation as a citizen to speak about political issues. You have a right to run your business in the way you believe is proper, because you have an obligation to run your business properly, not to neglect it. You have a right to raise your children in the way that you believe is best, because you have an obligation as a parent to raise your children in the way that is best.

Freedom of religion is the pattern for the other freedoms. You have a right to practice your religion according to the dictates of your conscience, because you have an obligation to practice your religion according to the dictates of your conscience. Classical liberalism bases our rights generally on our obligation to obey the dictates of our conscience.

This view of rights comes naturally to people who have the positive freedom to manage the serious work of society – to aristocrats who manage their own estates and serve in the Senate, or to smallholders who manage their own farms or businesses and make political decisions at town meetings. When you are managing this sort of important work, you obviously have an obligation to do a good job, and this is why you claim the right to do what you believe is a good job.

As we will see in the next chapter, the founders of the United States believed in a combination of this older moral liberalism and of the new self-interested Lockean liberalism. The abstract political philosophy that they used to claim their rights was based on Lockean social contract theory, the dominant popular political theory of their time, which Jefferson restated in the Declaration of Independence. But when they moved beyond these abstract political philosophy and decided which rights were important enough to protect in the Constitution and the Bill of Rights, the founders based this practical decision on classical liberal thought. The Constitution limited government to leave many responsibilities to voluntary associations, and it established a republican government with a division of powers and checks and balances, ideas about structure of government that are commonplaces of classical liberalism. The Bill of Rights protected citizens from government intrusion, and it protected freedom of speech, freedom of assembly, freedom of the press, and freedom of religion – the positive freedoms that let active citizens run their own society.

Chapter 3
Two Faces of Victorian Liberalism

In ancient Greece and Rome, republics were displaced by empires based on conquest of land, and in Renaissance Europe, monarchs built empires and claimed absolute power as they conquered the land of the new world. But when the industrial revolution arrived, manufacturing began to outweigh land as a source of wealth, so classical liberalism began to be eclipsed by new commercial values rather than by older aristocratic and monarchical values.

As the industrial revolution came to Britain, political philosophers developed a new commercial version of liberalism based on a new negative definition of freedom.

Classical liberalism has a positive idea of freedom: Freedom means the right to manage your own business affairs and your own government. This positive idea of freedom was shared by thinkers from Aristotle, who believed that only wealthy aristocrats could be free, to Jefferson, who believed that in a democratic nation of small property owners, everyone could be free.

After the industrial revolution, political philosophers adopted a new negative idea of freedom: Freedom means doing what you want without the government getting in your way. Positive freedom is freedom to manage your own life. Negative freedom is freedom from government interference.

This new negative definition of freedom let liberals support modernization as it eroded positive freedom. The market economy, which was the engine of modernization, was creating a class of life-long employees who would never run their own businesses, and it was making self-government more difficult, but laissez-faire liberals claimed that the market economy was increasing freedom, because it was based on voluntary contracts made without government interference. By arguing that any laws limiting the market were coercive, laissez-faire liberals helped nineteenth-century America to replace the old economy of independent smallholders with a modern industrial economy.

However, modernization was not yet complete during the nineteenth century: The family and voluntary local groups – such as churches and other charitable organizations – were still important economically. The market economy was based on self-interest, but it excluded women, who were supposed to have an unselfish nature that elevated the home, church and community. The woman's sphere was the realm outside of the market, where people still had positive freedom and were supposed to be motivated by high ideals, totally different from the selfish motives of the business world.

Conventional historians look only at the new commercial version of liberalism, but there was also another side of Victorian liberalism that was more high-minded and idealistic. Though laissez faire dominated liberal thinking on economics, the other side of Victorian liberalism was responsible for its most important social reforms – such as the abolition of slavery and feminism – and many of the reformers were women.

Laissez-faire liberals believed that people are economic animals, who have a natural right to pursue their self-interest. Idealist liberals of the nineteenth century kept alive the classical idea that people are moral animals, who have natural rights based on natural law and conscience.

Industrialization and Politics

After the Glorious Revolution of 1688, commercial interests were in firm control of the British government, and they transformed its economy.

Britain developed a modern banking system in 1697, when the government gave the Bank of England a monopoly on joint-stock banking in exchange for the Bank's creating a "funded debt" for the government – a debt with no fixed payment date, which creditors could sell to other investors when they wanted their money back. The Bank of England's monopoly status made it a reserve bank, whose notes were considered so trustworthy that other banks kept them to back their own notes instead of keeping reserves of gold.[69] The funded debt gave commercial interests a permanent stake in the government's stability. A reserve bank could expand the money supply to promote economic growth.

Parliamentary corruption became very common after the Glorious Revolution: Ministers of the Crown found they could no longer coerce Parliament, but they could control it by offering money and offering positions in the government and in the Church of England to members who voted properly. Corruption reached its high point under the government of Robert Walpole, Great Britain's most powerful politician from 1721 to 1742, who was the first minister of the British government to be called "Prime Minister" and to live at 10 Downing St. Walpole kept a secret fund to buy votes and to subsidize journals that supported his point of view, he gave political plums to his relatives as well as to his supporters in Parliament, and he invented the saying, "Every man has his price."

Britain's economy industrialized gradually. From the Renaissance through the eighteenth century, landlords continued to enclose the commons, driving people into cities where they worked in factories for subsistence wages, making Britain the workshop of the world.

As it industrialized, Britain created a society that still seems familiar to us, though it now seems old fashioned – a society where middle-class men supported their families by going to work in offices, where working-class men supported their families by going to work in factories, and where women stayed at home with the children.

Hamiltonians and Jeffersonians

In Britain, commercial interests were firmly in control after the glorious revolution, but in America, there was a prolonged political battle about modernization.

The Federalists, led by Alexander Hamilton, represented commercial interests that supported modernization. They wanted the states to unite under a national government that would establish a sound currency and promote commerce. They also supported a tariff on imported goods to promote domestic manufacturing.

The anti-federalists and Democratic Republicans, led by Thomas Jefferson, represented smallholders and agrarian interests that opposed modernization. At first, they opposed a stronger federal government. After the constitution created a stronger federal government, they opposed a national bank, because they wanted to slow down the money economy to preserve an economy of small independent farmers. They supported free trade, hoping that America could avoid industrialization by exporting agricultural goods and importing manufactured goods from Europe.

There were two reasons for the differences between the Hamiltonians and the Jeffersonians. The first is still an important issue, the distribution of wealth: Jeffersonians believed that industrialization would increase inequality and so undermine democracy. The second, as Michael Sandel has said, was considered more important at the time but is no longer a political issue today, the moral effect of modernization:[70] Jeffersonians believed that industrialization would create a small class of wealthy people, who were devoted to luxury and self-interest rather than to the public good, and a large class of workers who were dependent and servile. Looking at Britain, where moneyed interests controlled the government, the Jeffersonians believed that we had to resist modernization to preserve democracy.

Behind these differences were two different versions of liberalism.

Jeffersonians believed in classical liberalism. In their view, democracy was essentially a moral enterprise: It had to create citizens with the character needed for economic independence and self-government.

Hamiltonians believed in a newer version of liberalism based on harnessing self-interest. As Hamilton said, "Our prevailing passions are ambition and interest; and it will ever be the duty of a wise government to avail itself of these passions, in order to make them subservient to the public good."[71]

Hamilton thought of himself as a representative of commercial modernity, rather than of virtuous antiquity,[72] and he realized that his policies would have the results that the Jeffersonians feared, saying:

... as riches increase and accumulate in few hands; as luxury prevails in society; virtue will be in greater degree considered only a graceful appendage of wealth, and the tendency of things will be to depart from the republican standard. This is the real disposition of human nature.... It is a common misfortune, that awaits our state constitution as well as all others.[73]

Hamilton admitted that trade and manufacturing would lead to corruption, as the Jeffersonians said, but he believed that this change was inevitable – and events proved him right.

The Bank and Manufacturing

The battle over modernization between the Hamiltonians and Jeffersonians centered on two issues: whether there should be a Bank of the United States and whether the country should encourage manufacturing. Hamilton supported a Bank of the United States, modeled on the Bank of England, to promote economic growth and to link "the interest of the State in an intimate connection with those of the rich individuals belonging to it."[74] In his *Report on Public Credit* of 1790, he recommended that the federal government assume the states' debts, for the same reasons. The bank and national debt were modeled on Britain's economic policies, and Jeffersonians believed they would undermine democracy by bringing the same sort of corruption to the United States that Walpole had brought to England. At one point, Hamilton said that the British government worked only because of corruption, and Jefferson remarked that "Hamilton was not only a monarchist but for a monarchy bottomed on corruption."[75]

The United States established a Bank, but it did not adopt the second recommendation of the Hamiltonians, the plan for government subsidies to manufacturing recommended in Hamilton's Report on Manufacturing of 1791. Jeffersonians were in favor of household manufacturing but against factories in commercial cities. Jefferson wrote about the "depravity of morals, dependence, and corruption"[76] of Europe's great manufacturing cities, and he believed that self-government was impossible for the degraded working class that existed in Birmingham or Manchester.

Yet Jefferson inadvertently stimulated American manufacturing when he declared an embargo on imports in 1807, in order to avoid becoming entangled in the war between Britain and France. Britain's blockade of American trade during the War of 1812 also stimulated manufacturing and showed how dangerous it was to rely on imported goods. In 1816, Jefferson wrote, "experience has taught me that manufactures are now as necessary to our independence as to our comfort."[77] By this time, the older party differences were disappearing, as everyone accepted the realities of a modern commercial economy: James Madison, a leading opponent of the First Bank twenty-five years earlier, approved the establishment of the Second Bank in 1816.

Some of the old Jeffersonian ideas were revived in the 1830s: Andrew Jackson vetoed the renewal of the Bank's charter and tried to require that all payments of less than $20 be made in specie rather than in banknotes. These hard-money policies were meant to slow the economy, and they were accompanied by impassioned Jeffersonian rhetoric: Samuel Beardsley thundered in the House of Representatives that, if credit and commerce depended on the Bank, then "I, for one, say perish credit; perish commerce; ... give us a broken, a deranged, and a worthless currency, rather than the ignoble and corrupting tyranny of an irresponsible corporation."[78]

Yet the Jacksonian coalition that opposed the Bank of the United States was split by a fundamental difference over economic policy. Jacksonians in the commercial cities of the East saw that manufacturing was creating a degraded working class that threatened the status of independent workers; groups such as the New England Association of Farmers, Mechanics and Other Workingmen hoped that hard money would discourage further industrialization.[79] But Jacksonians in the West were prospering by buying and selling land and farm products, and they did not have an industrial working class near at hand as a warning about the future. They opposed the Bank of the United States only because it sent their money back East, and they wanted their state banks to create paper money to stimulate commerce. As it happened, Jackson stopped the Bank of the United States, but state banks kept creating money more quickly than ever: Easy money fueled a speculative boom during the Jackson years, which led to a crash as Van Buren was beginning his term.

The Jeffersonian and Jacksonian resistance to the industrial economy were put to rest in 1840, when the Whig William Henry Harrison was elected president. Harrison was a man of the people who was born in a log cabin, and he formed a new majority by uniting the commercial interests of the East with Westerners – who were hungry for prosperity and had supported Jackson only because he represented the common man while the Federalists represented the aristocracy. After 1840, there were still attempts to help people escape from industrialization and become economically independent in the West – such as the Free Soil movement and the

Homestead Act – but the fight to stop manufacturing and commerce had ended.⁸⁰

By the 1840s, Americans had reconciled themselves to the fact that the country had an urban working class, people who would spend their lives as other men's employees and never own their own businesses. Later in the nineteenth century, the industrial model spread to the frontier. The workers in businesses that produced beef for the national market were called "cowboys" all their lives, to distinguish them from the "cowmen" who owned the businesses. They were life-long employees, boys rather than men, unlike the independent family farmers who had settled the east.

Liberalism and Self-Interest

Economic relations were still personal in England at the time of the Puritan rebellion and in America at the time of the American revolution. The business owner worked in the same shop as his employees, and the seller lived in the same town as the buyer. There was not a sharp distinction between personal life and business, and both were supposed to be governed by the same moral code.

Industrialization created an impersonal economy based on large-scale production. The business owner hardly knew the men who worked for him, and goods were sold to distant consumers, so business became impersonal and distinct from one's private life. At home, people were still part of a family, neighborhood, and church, but when they did business, people were isolated individuals pursuing their own interests.

Reflecting this economic change, political theories that assume people are motivated by individual self-interest became prominent in seventeenth-century Britain and became dominant by the nineteenth century.

The Social Contract

The social contract was the first political theory of the new self-interested version of liberalism that began to develop in seventeenth century Britain. This theory holds that individuals in the state of nature pursued their own interests in conflict with each other, and that these individuals decided to join together and create a state in order to reduce conflict and let them pursue their own interests more effectively. It assumed that people had the same motivations in the state of nature, before society was created, as the self-interested economic men who appeared after industrialization created an impersonal market economy.[81]

Robinson Crusoe is the seventeenth century's most striking image of the new economic man. Even though he was stranded on a desert island and cut off from other people, Crusoe is supposed to have lived a model life because he worked hard and provided himself with abundant food, a comfortable house, and the other trappings of prosperity.

Once we see man as an economic rather than a moral and political animal, it begins to seem that natural law and natural rights are two totally different things. If you begin with the classical view that human nature is essentially moral, then there is not a sharp distinction between natural law and natural rights: People want freedom in order to act morally, and so natural rights derive from natural law. But if you begin with the view that human nature is essentially economic, then the natural rights that people demand to pursue their self-interest are entirely different from their moral obligations under natural law.

Thomas Hobbes

It is not a coincidence that Thomas Hobbes, the first major philosopher to develop social contract theory, was also the first to say that natural rights are the opposite of natural law – and to criticize earlier philosophers for "confusing" them:

> though they that speak of the subject use to confound ius and lex, rights and law: yet they ought to be distinguished; because RIGHT consisteth in liberty to do, or to forbear: whereas LAW determineth and bindeth to one of them: so that law and right differ as much, as do obligation and liberty. [82]

Hobbes is saying here that natural rights involve freedom to do whatever we please, so they are the opposite of the natural law that tells us what we should do. By contrast, classical liberals believed that natural rights give us the freedom to do what the natural laws tell us we should do.

Because conventional history identifies liberalism with self-interested individualism and the social contract, Hobbes is widely considered an early exponent of some liberal ideas, so it is necessary to belabor the obvious fact that Hobbes believed in absolute, authoritarian government, because he thought that an all-powerful state could most effectively guarantee security and prosperity.

Let's look at a few examples of how strongly he rejects fundamental liberal principles. Hobbes believed that sovereignty was indivisible: That is, there should not be a separation of powers between the executive and legislature or between church and state. Hobbes believed that the sovereign must be above the law, because he creates the law, so he cannot not be accused of injustice by his subjects, and he cannot forfeit the loyalty of his subjects by acting unjustly. Hobbes believed the sovereign should have the power to punish and reward his subjects arbitrarily, "according to the law he hath formerly made, or if there be no law made, according as he shall judge" good for the commonwealth; that is Hobbes opposed the idea that there should be a government of laws, not of men. In all these cases, he opposed liberal principles that had been familiar ideas of political philosophy since the time of Aristotle or of Thomas Aquinas.

Hobbes also opposed free speech, saying that the sovereign should:

> be judge of what opinions and doctrines are averse, and what conducing to peace; and consequently, on what occasions, and how far, and what men are to be trusted withal, in speaking to multitudes of people; and who shall examine the doctrines of all books before they be published. For the actions of men proceed from their opinions; and in the well-governing of opinions, consisteth the well-governing of men's actions....[83]

Hobbes is called an early exponent of liberal theory because he said people make the social contract to preserve their lives so the government does not have a right to take their lives, implying that the power of government is limited by the purpose for which people formed it. In fact, Hobbes said a subject could legitimately disobey the sovereign only if he asked the subject to kill or wound himself – because people entered into the social contract to preserve their lives and safety – but he also said that the sovereign has the right to take the life of the subject whenever he believes it is good for the commonwealth, with or without the law on his side, though the subject is not obligated to cooperate with him.[84]

Hobbes is far less liberal than Harrington, Milton, and other writers of his time, and is also less liberal than the main tradition of classical philosophy, as he himself says:

> In these western parts of the world, we are made to receive our opinions concerning the rights of commonwealths, from Aristotle, Cicero, and other men, Greeks and Romans, that living under popular states, derived those rights ... out of the practices of their own commonwealths, which were popular .... And by reading these Greek and Latin authors, men from their childhood have gotten a habit, under a false show of liberty, of favoring tumults, and of licentious controlling the actions of their sovereigns ....[85]

Though conventional history considers him a forerunner of liberalism, this quotation shows that Hobbes himself knew that he was far less liberal than earlier philosophers.

Reading Hobbes should make it very clear that self-interest and social contract theory do not add up to liberalism. For example, Hobbes is perfectly logical when he uses his theories to justify censorship of dangerous ideas: If people form a government to protect their self-interest, then they should suppress speech that threatens their self-interest.

Hobbes believed in pure social contract theory: There is no right or wrong before the contract.[86] This theory implies that there is nothing wrong with gratuitous cruelty to animals, since animals cannot make a contract agreeing that they will not to be cruel to us. It also implies that if we discover other groups of people, as the Europeans did when they discovered America, we may either slaughter and exploit them or make a contract with them, whichever is to our advantage – since we have no moral obligation to them before we make a contract.[87]

John Locke

John Locke was the first to use the social contract as the basis of a liberal political theory. His writing combined elements of natural law with social contract theory, in contrast to Hobbes' pure social contract theory.

Locke argued that people have a natural right to defend their life, liberty and property, that they established a social contract in order to create a government that protects their natural rights, that governments should be limited to the powers that are needed to protect these rights,[88] and that if a government does not protect these rights, citizens may dissolve it and establish a new government.[89]

As the basis of his theory of natural rights, Locke says man in the state of nature has a right to his property because he creates and accumulates this property by mixing his labor with what nature offers; because his labor is his property, anything that his labor is intermixed with is also his property.[90] In this theory of natural rights, the moral and political man of classical liberalism is replaced by economic man whose interest is accumulating property, and liberal theory moves from moral individualism to self-interested individualism.

In the *Second Treatise*, Locke's most important work on politics, he says a government can be dissolved only if it violates people's "property" – a word that Locke uses to mean their "Lives, Liberties and Estates"[91] – in other words, if it violates their natural right to pursue their self interest. The *Second Treatise* does not mention freedom of speech, freedom of the press or freedom of religion.[92]

Locke contradicted himself, because he was a transitional figure who combined the old natural law theory with the new social contract theory. His two most important books were the *Second Treatise*, with its theory of natural rights, and the *Essay Concerning Human Understanding*, which argued that all knowledge is based on sense experience. But his belief in natural rights, which looks back to classical philosophy, contradicts his empiricism, which anticipates later English philosophy. It is impossible to derive natural rights from sense experience – you cannot see or touch a right. Locke may have understood this contradiction,[93] and philosophers all understood it a century later, after Hume carried Locke's empiricism to its logical conclusion and showed that it had no room for self-evident rights.[94]

The contradictions in Locke's thinking were handed down to his followers, to Voltaire and other Enlightenment philosophers who thought Locke provided a scientific basis for liberal politics.[95] Because historians usually trace liberalism to these transitional thinkers, who combine some elements of the older natural law theory with some elements of the new empiricism and scientism, they do not see how sharp the contrast is between classical moral liberalism and the purely self-interested liberalism of the nineteenth century.

Laissez Faire and Liberty

There were also political theorists in eighteenth century Britain who went further than these transitional figures by abandoning natural law completely and arguing that society could be based solely on self-interest, and this view became dominant in the nineteenth century.

Some claimed that an authoritarian government could coordinate individuals' conflicting interests, as Hobbes had: This was David Hume's bias in his *History of England* (1754-1761).

Others claimed that self-interested behavior could automatically coordinate itself. For example, Bernard Mandeville wrote in the *Fable of the Bees* (1724) that "private vices" automatically bring "public benefits," because people who indulge their taste for luxuries create work for tradesmen and manufacturers, increasing everyone's prosperity.[96] And Adam Smith famously wrote in *The Wealth of Nations* (1776) that, if everyone is free to pursue his self-interest, the "invisible hand" of the market will promote the common good.

Following Adam Smith, economists and utilitarian philosophers developed an empiricist version of liberalism. They abandoned Locke's idea of natural rights, and instead based their theory on the empirically observable fact that people seek pleasure and avoid pain.

Their theory is familiar to anyone who has studied basic economic textbooks that begin by summarizing this underlying principle of laissez-faire. If people can choose freely what they produce and consume, each person will maximize his or her own satisfaction; it follows that any government action that prevents people from choosing freely forces them to consume products that give them less satisfaction than the product they would have chosen for themselves. This basic principle underlying free-market economic theory assumes that people are rational agents who try to maximize their own satisfaction.

If we base a theory of civil liberties on the same view of human nature, we will conclude that we should let everyone make the choices that maximize their own satisfaction, up to the point where they prevent other people from pursuing their satisfaction. The most famous statement of this idea of civil liberties is John Stuart Mill's *On Liberty*.[97] Mill's idea of civil liberties – that people should be free to do anything that they want, as long as they do not harm or interfere with the freedom of anyone else – follows logically from the laissez-faire view of man as a self-interested satisfaction maximizer.

Mill's *On Liberty* is sometimes called the classic statement of liberalism. It is admired by our conservatives, who want to minimize government, and by our liberals, who do not want the law to forbid any behavior of "consenting adults." It seems to expand freedom as much as possible: Its broad principle, that you have a right to do anything you choose unless you hurt someone else, seems to go beyond the classic liberal ideals of freedom of speech, freedom of religion and other rights that only protect specific activities. But this principle actually weakens the classical ideal of freedom in two important ways.

First, this laissez-faire view of liberty does not give us any reason to stop the authorities from suppressing "dangerous" speech or religious practices. For example, the Catholic church prevented Galileo from saying that the earth revolved around the sun on the grounds that unsettling our view of the universe would cause religious and social disorder, and conservatives argued during the Protestant reformation that an established church was absolutely necessary to social stability. The powers that be have always justified censorship and religious coercion by saying that they are needed to protect society, and Mill's theory does not give us any argument against them.

Mill himself always defended freedom of speech and of religion, but that was because he wanted to retain the earlier victories of liberalism – not because his utilitarian theory of liberalism supported these freedoms. He begins *On Liberty* by saying that freedom of speech should be absolute and that he will examine the limits of freedom of action, which can never be absolute but should be expanded as much as possible. Yet there is no basis in his utilitarian philosophy for the idea that freedom of speech should be absolute. Free speech should be absolute if our loyalty to the truth transcends our loyalty to our own comfort, but there is no room in utilitarianism for this sort of transcendent ideal. Utilitarians believe that there are no values beyond the experiences of pleasure and pain; if they were consistent, they would illegalize ideas that hurt people, just as they illegalize actions that hurt people. Hobbes believed that a society should suppress ideas that would reduce its total pleasure or increase its total pain, and utilitarians should believe the same thing – but fortunately, they were not consistent about this issue and did not actually reduce freedom of speech and of religion.

Second, this laissez-faire theory of liberty undermines our freedom to govern ourselves. It restricts freedom to private decisions. It expects the market to take care of the public realm, and it says government must not interfere with people's choices in the market.

This is how laissez-faire liberalism actually reduced freedom. It gave people more freedom to pursue their private interests, but it reduced their freedom to act politically. For example, according to laissez-faire theory, even if nine-tenths of the people in a town do not want a railroad station built there, they cannot legitimately stop the station. It should be built, as long as the 10 percent who want the railroad in town can give it enough business to make it profitable. Whether the railroad comes to town is a private affair between the railroad's owners and its customers, and a law keeping the railroad out of town would interfere with their freedom of choice. Though it is very obvious that building the railroad station would change the character of the town completely and affect everyone who lives there, laissez-faire liberalism ignores these effects of private decisions on the public realm.

Mill wrote *On Liberty* in 1859, when Britain was fighting the second Opium War to overturn Chinese laws that prevented British businesses from importing opium from India. The British said these laws were illegitimate because they interfered with free trade. Chinese negotiators agreed to legalize the sale of opium in 1858; *On Liberty* was published in 1859, and the British and French captured Peking in 1860 to force China to observe the free-trade agreement. Opium was so destructive to Chinese society, and the British and French victory was so humiliating, that Chairman Mao undoubtedly had the memory of the opium wars in the back of his mind a century later, when he decided to close China to all trade with the outside world. But the British believed that they were fighting this war to extend English economic freedoms to China – not that they were interfering with China's right to self-government.

Laissez-faire liberals redefined liberty as purely negative freedom, as each individual's right to do what they please without interference from the government. This new idea of liberty eroded the positive freedom of communities to govern themselves, and it promoted the economic modernization that eroded the positive freedom of people to run their own small businesses.

Liberalism and Idealism

You would expect that there would be a drastic moral decline during the Victorian period, if people really believed that the goal of life was to maximize your own satisfaction and that the law should not stop people from gratifying themselves by any means, including opium. Could utilitarianism and laissez-faire economics really have been the ideologies of the age that is famous for its Victorian morality?

Laissez-faire liberals (like today's conservatives) claimed that the discipline of the market was morally bracing. They opposed welfare and social insurance, and they believed the market would force people to think about their long-term self-interest, not just about the pleasure of the moment – or they would end up on the streets. But market discipline does not explain Victorian morality. For one thing, there were more private charities in the nineteenth century than people today realize, which reduced the "morally bracing" discipline of the market: John Stuart Mill called them a "great and continually increasing mass of unenlightened and shortsighted benevolence," run by women who were too soft-headed to realize that they were undermining morality.[98] More important, the discipline of the market obviously does not explain why even Victorians who were independently wealthy – all the people you read about in Victorian novels who have property worth 500 pounds per year or more – generally wanted to be respectable rather than to live as hedonists. – pleasure seeker

The key to Victorian morality is the life that went on outside of the market economy, in the family, church, and community. When Hobbes, Locke or Adam Smith said that society was made up of self-interested individuals, they were thinking of adult males, who were the heads of households and who competed in the market economy to support their families. A woman's place was in the home, where people were supposed to live by totally different values. The economy was based on self-interest, but marriage was supposed to be based on love, and within your home, you were supposed to be devoted to your loved ones with total selflessness.

Public and Private Life

At the time of the industrial revolution, the English began to think of personal life as something totally separate from public life.

Before the industrial revolution, the Protestants had already put a new emphasis on personal life. As work at home replaced collective agricultural work on the manor, religion began to emphasize personal conscience rather than collective rituals. Personal life became more important, but it was not totally separate from public life. Artisans' homes were connected to their workshops, and they had an obligation to treat apprentices as members of their families. The mistress of the house cooked for everyone, and the master was responsible for his apprentices' religious training. The guilds were almost an extension of the family, providing help such as insurance for their members, and city governments were based on the guilds. Radical Protestants had a new sense of moral earnestness about their family lives, but they had the same sense of moral earnestness about their work and their politics.

A different idea of personal life became widespread as work moved to offices and factories separated from the home, where work was part of a competitive economy based on the impersonal laws of the market. When it came to economic affairs, your behavior had to be coldly self-interested, or your business would not survive. The economy was cold and impersonal, and personal satisfactions were available outside of the economy, in your private and family life. It was best to move your family to suburbs that were physically distant from your workplace. Children had to be shielded from harsh economic realities. The family was a "haven in a heartless world": The Victorians became famous for sentimentalizing the family, because its warmth stood out in such sharp contrast with their impersonal, competitive economy.

Laissez-faire economic theory focuses exclusively on the satisfactions that people get from consuming the commodities that the economy produces. But in reality, middle-class Victorians looked at economic life as a means to the more high-minded satisfactions of family life.

The separation of work from the home led to the cult of domesticity, to the child-centered family, and to the roles for men and women that were considered normal until the mid-twentieth century. Women were supposed to devote their time to family, church, and voluntary organizations such as charities, rather than working in the market economy. Victorians idealized women, "put them up on a pedestal," because they were more pure, spiritual and selfless than men; but this attitude also downgraded women, since everyone knew that the rough, competitive world of men was where the big decisions were made.

At the time, the family was still important economically because the modern economy had not developed so thoroughly that it took over all the work of the home. The family still had most of the responsibility for raising children. It was still responsible for basic production, such as baking, mending, and making clothing. It was responsible for most entertainment and leisure activity: Every cultivated woman was expected to know how to play the piano. And the family, along with the church and other voluntary groups, was also responsible for most charity, because laissez-faire liberals believed the state should do as little as possible for the poor.

Louisa May Alcott's *Little Women* gives us a good picture of a Victorian family's productive activities. They pull Amy out of school and teach her at home, because they do not approve of her teacher. They put on plays at home to entertain themselves. Though they themselves are economically pressed, they make sacrifices to help feed and nurse a poor, sick family. During the Victorian period, the family still did real work – and this work was supposed to be motivated by love within the family and by charity outside of the family, not by self-interest.

Idealist Philosophy

The two main schools of nineteenth-century philosophy, empiricism and idealism, seem to reflect these two sides of Victorian economic life. On the one hand, empiricism says that all knowledge is based on experience, so we cannot have any knowledge of transcendent moral ideals: The utilitarians were empiricists, and their ethical theory is based on experienced pleasure and pain. As empiricism reflects the values of the market economy, the rival philosophy of idealism seems to reflect the values of the Victorian home – very high-minded but a bit out of touch with material realities.

Kant

Transcendental idealism began with Immanuel Kant, who believed he proved that a "noumenal" world exists beyond the world of sense experience but that we cannot have any knowledge of it. Politically, Kant was liberal for his time and place, an admirer of the Enlightenment and of Frederick the Great,[99] who brought the Enlightenment to Prussia. Though he believed that citizens should always obey the authorities, he thought that history would move gradually toward a free society as rulers gave their people freedom:

> ... freedom spreads by degrees. When the citizen is hindered in seeking his own welfare in his own way, so long as it is consistent with the freedom of others, the vitality of the entire enterprise is sapped, and therewith the powers of the whole are diminished. Therefore limitations on personal action are removed, and general religious freedom is permitted. Enlightenment comes gradually....[100]

In Kant's view, the best government is a republic with power divided between legislative, executive, and judicial branches.[101] Under this sort of government, individuals will support just laws, because the laws they make will apply equally to everyone, including themselves.[102]

Hegel

In central Europe, idealism was spread by the Hegelians, who used it to justify authoritarian government. Hegel believed that the state is the culmination of the spirit's movement toward self-realization in history, and because freedom is the power to realize yourself, the truly free person is one who identifies with the state: "Freedom is merely to know and understand such general and substantial matters as law and right, to will them and to create a reality which suits them – the state."[103] Likewise, Hegel says:

The state does not exist for the citizens; on the contrary, one could say that the state is the end and they are its means. But the means-end relation is not fitting here. For the state is not the abstract confronting the citizens; they are parts of it, like members of an organic body, where no member is end and none is means. It is the realization of Freedom, of the absolute, final purpose, and exists for its own sake. All the value man has, all spiritual reality, he has only through the state. ... The state is the divine idea as it exists on earth."[104]

Because of Hegel's influence, many philosophers came to identify idealism with authoritarianism,[105] but this identification is not true of most strands of nineteenth-century idealism.

American Transcendentalists

Idealism influenced America through the writing of Emerson and the transcendentalists, who were liberals. In Emerson's view, political reforms – from the Protestant reformation to the American revolution to the anti-slavery movement of his own day – were based on idealism, not on self interest: "The history of reform is always identical, it is the comparison of the idea with the fact. Our modes of living are not agreeable to our imagination. We suspect they are unworthy."[106] Movements for reform educate our consciences by exposing us to higher ideals.[107]

Like Milton, Emerson believed that freedom was important because of its moral value:

> Wild liberty develops iron conscience. Want of liberty, by strengthening law and decorum, stupefies conscience.[108]

Emerson was an individualist – he wrote that "the nation exists for the individual"[109] – but, as we can see in this quotation about liberty and conscience, he believed in moral individualism rather than self-interested individualism.

The Transcendentalists were among the leaders of the great liberal movements of nineteenth century America. New England, particularly Boston, was still influenced by radical Protestantism even after it became industrialized, and it was different politically from the rest of the country.[110] Its culture in 1886, when Henry James wrote *The Bostonians*, does not seem very different from its culture in Emerson's time: There is the same moral earnestness, the same passion for political reform (though emancipation of women replaced emancipation of the slaves as the main issue after the Civil War), the same idealism and vague spiritualism, the same appetite for high-minded, long-winded lectures.

Women have an important place in this culture in James' novel, as they did in Emerson's time. The gathering place for young reformers in the novel is the home of Miss Birdseye, an elderly Bostonian who dedicated a long life to reform: She had "spent a month in a Georgian jail" while she roamed through the South carrying the Bible to the slaves; she had preached temperance "in Irish circles, where the doctrine was received with missiles"; and she had taken abandoned children off the streets "to her own poor rooms." Despite all the years that had gone by and all the hardships she had gone through, "the only thing that was still actual to her was the elevation of the species by the reading of Emerson ...."[111]

The transcendentalist Thoreau invented the phrase "civil disobedience," continuing Thomas Aquinas' idea that we have an obligation to disobey unjust laws, and anticipating Gandhi and Martin Luther King. Civil disobedience is based on the idea that we must disobey unjust laws because we have an obligation to a higher law. There is no basis for it in self-interested liberalism. It derives from the natural law tradition of classical liberalism.

Transcendentalism does not fit into the conventional history of liberalism, which considers only the commercial Lockean and laissez-faire liberalism of the seventeenth through nineteenth century and the modernist liberalism of the twentieth century.

For one thing, this important strain of American liberal thinking was explicitly anti-Lockean. Emerson wrote:

> ... the idealism of the present day acquired the name of Transcendental from the use of that term by Immanuel Kant, of Konigsberg, who replied to the skeptical philosophy of Locke, which insisted that there was nothing in the intellect which was not previously in the experience of the senses ....[112]

For another thing, this strain of liberalism questioned technological progress and the market economy. Emerson wrote:

> Machinery is aggressive. The weaver becomes a web, the machinist a machine. If you do not use the tools, they use you.... What have these arts done for the character, for the worth of mankind? Are men better? 'Tis sometimes questioned whether morals have not declined as the arts have ascended. Here are great arts and little men.....[113]

As this quotation shows, Emerson's ideas do not fit into the conventional view of nineteenth-century American liberalism, which ties it to commercial values and economic growth. Of course, Emerson's disciple Thoreau became famous for rejecting commercial values and economic growth in favor of simple living and high-minded thinking.

Economic and Social Liberalism

When Emerson speaks of an economy that would produce fewer goods but would produce freer and better men, he is in the tradition of Jefferson, but limiting modernization was no longer a live political issue in the 1840s, as it had been in Jefferson's day. The Jeffersonians had practical economic policies that they hoped would create an economy with fewer goods but with freer men, while Emerson had this ideal but had no practical economic policies to go with it.

Emerson recognized that the people of his time were powerless to change the direction of the economy. He wrote: "A terrible machine has possessed itself of the ground, the air, and the men and women, and hardly even thought is free," and he said the same thing more concisely in his famous statement, "Things are in the saddle and ride mankind."[114]

Likewise, Thoreau criticized the new technologies of his time – he wrote "We do not ride on the railroad; it rides upon us"[115] – but he dropped out of the economy to live at Walden Pond, rather than trying to change the economy.

In practice, laissez-faire liberals dominated thinking about economics during the Victorian age, while idealist liberals worked on social issues, such as abolition and women's suffrage. The idealists worked to extend freedom to groups that had been excluded, but they could not stop industrialization from eroding everyone's positive freedom, as the market economy did more and more things that people used to do for themselves.

Idealists as Reformers in America

Because their role in the history of liberalism has been neglected, we should review the contributions that philosophical and religious idealists made to the abolitionist and feminist movements, which were supported primarily by Transcendentalists, Evangelical Protestants, members of the old radical Protestant sects, such as the Quakers and Congregationalists, and members of liberal Protestant denominations, such as the Unitarians.

"Abolitionism," Richard Hofstadter says, "was a religious movement, emerging from the ferment of evangelical Protestantism, psychologically akin to other reforms – women's rights, temperance, and pacifism"[116]: He calls it a "moral frenzy" among middle-class northerners who did not have an economic interest in preserving or ending slavery.

The Quakers were the first to mount an organized campaign against slavery. During the second half of the eighteenth century, Quaker leaders such as George Fox in England and John Woolman in the United States, preached that spiritual freedom to obey God and conscience required freedom to act on your beliefs in this world. Slavery was a form of moral imprisonment that prevented people from choosing the good.

Among American abolitionist leaders, John Greenleaf Whittier was a Quaker. Wendell Phillips was a Boston transcendentalist. Levi Coffin, called the "President of the Underground Railroad," was a Quaker. Theodore Parker was a Unitarian pastor in Boston. Theodore Weld began by studying to become a minister at Lane Theological

Seminary. Harriet Beecher Stowe was the daughter of Lyman Beecher, the president of Lane Theological Seminary. Henry Ward Beecher was the son of Lyman Beecher and was a Congregationalist minister. William Lloyd Garrison was a Christian "perfectionist" – an evangelical movement that believed in abolitionism, women's rights, pacifism, and the need to "come out" of a corrupt society by refusing to obey its laws (another version of civil disobedience).

In a famous incident in the history of abolitionism, students at Lane Theological Seminary, in Cincinnati, founded a society to discuss the issue of slavery in 1833 and passed resolutions calling for immediate emancipation. When a public outcry pressured the Board of Trustees to ban the student anti-slavery society, a group of the seminarians proclaimed:

> Free discussion, being a duty, is consequently a right, and as such is inherent and inalienable. It is *our* right. It *was* before we entered Lane Seminary.... this *right* the institution could neither give nor take away.[117]

Despite social contract theory, the seminarian's statement shows that the classical liberal idea that our natural rights are based on our moral obligations was still very much alive in nineteenth century America.

Like the abolitionist leaders, the most important feminist leaders were transcendentalists and radical or liberal Protestants. The Grimke Sisters converted to Quakerism before becoming active in the anti-slavery and women's rights movement. Lucretia Mott was born a Quaker and became a Quaker minister at the age of 28. Elizabeth Cady Stanton was raised in a strict Calvinistic family, was deeply affected by the Evangelical movement and then by the Quakerism of Lucretia Mott, and she joined the transcendentalists' circle when her husband moved to Boston to practice law. Margaret Fuller was a Boston transcendentalist, coeditor with Emerson of *The Dial*, whom the other Bostonians admired because she had read the idealist philosophers in the original German. Susan B. Anthony was raised as a Hicksite (liberal) Quaker, and after she married, she and her husband became Unitarians. Amelia Bloomer was raised as a Quaker.

(The only important nineteenth century feminists who were not religious or philosophical idealists were Victoria and Tennessee Woodhull, sisters whose father was a traveling healer who peddled an "elixir of life." When they reached New York, the aged and sickly Commodore Vanderbilt was attracted by their reputation as healers and set them up as stockbrokers. In 1870, they began publishing a magazine that carried financial news and articles on spiritualism, women's rights, birth control, and free love. They were known for opposing the double-standard of sexual morality, but unlike Susan B. Anthony, who wanted to raise men to the women's standard, they wanted women to have the same sexual freedom as men: Victoria said that she had the "inalienable right" to have as many lovers as she pleased.[118] This version of feminism was produced by the entrepreneurial side of Victorian America at its worst – by snake-oil vendors financed by a robber baron – and it was very different from mainstream Victorian feminism. But ideas like the Woodhulls' became mainstream in the twentieth century, when the market economy dominated the country more completely: Their magazine was the first to offer the combination of sexual liberation and advice about how to get ahead that filled the women's magazines by the 1960s.)

Idealists as Reformers in Britain

In Great Britain, as in America, most social reformers were idealists. For example, Quakers formed the Abolition Society in 1787. William Wilberforce, whom the British credit with abolishing slavery, was elected to Parliament in 1780 but did not devote himself to abolition until after he converted to Evangelical Christianity.

Evangelicals led the reform movement in early nineteenth century Britain, and they fought for abolitionism and temperance. They aimed to make the Establishment worthy of its power, not to do away with the Establishment, and their politics was sometimes called "Liberal Toryism."

Groups outside of the Establishment became more influential later in the nineteenth century, particularly during the 1860s, when there were widespread revival meetings among Methodists and Nonconformists. Nonconformist societies helped Gladstone's Liberals gain a Parliamentary majority in 1868, at a time when the political battle lines of the time were drawn between Nonconformist religion and the established Church and landed aristocracy. One historian has said, "the Nonconformists were the only important policy-makers in the [Liberal] party, apart from Gladstone himself."[119]

Philosophical idealism influenced English liberalism in the late nineteenth century. Though empiricism dominated British philosophy during most of the nineteenth century, idealism became important later in the century, and the neo-Hegelian idealist, T. H. Green, was the most important liberal political theorist in Britain between 1880 and World War I. Green wrote when parliament was passing reforms such as the compulsory education laws and factory acts that guaranteed safe working conditions, which laissez-faire liberals considered a violation of freedom of contract.

Green attacked John Stuart Mill's laissez-faire idea of freedom by calling it "negative freedom," as this book does. By contrast, he advocated positive freedom, freedom to realize your better self, to do something worth doing. Though they are free from government interference, he said, factory workers do not have positive freedom if they have no education and must work in conditions that destroy their health.

Green said that government should create conditions that let people act independently, and he added that his idea that the government should act to promote positive freedom did not justify authoritarian or paternalistic government:

> The true ground of objection to "paternal government" is not that it violates the "laissez-faire" principle and conceives that its office is to make people good, to promote morality, but that it rests on a misconception of morality. The real function of government being to maintain conditions of life in which morality shall be possible, and morality consisting in the disinterested performance of self-imposed duties, "paternal government" does its best to make it impossible by narrowing the room for the self-imposition of duties and for the play of disinterested motives.[120]

Like Milton and Emerson, Green believed in freedom because he believed that actions have no moral value unless they are performed freely.

Victorian Hypocrisy

Because Victorian society was split between the world of business and the world of the family, Victorians became famous for their hypocrisy. The behavior accepted among men in the market was not even mentioned in the family or in the "mixed company" of men and women.

Nowadays, we often talk about how strict Victorian morality was, but we tend to forget how Victorians behaved in the market.

For example, we blame the Victorians for repressing sex, but they were quite willing to tolerate prostitution – sex in the market economy, removed from the family. France legalized prostitution in 1785 as a public health measure, and elegant Parisian houses of prostitution, such as Maxim's, were famous world-wide during the nineteenth century. In Victorian Britain and America, prostitution was illegal, but the authorities tolerated red light districts. In some American cities, there were fixed fines, which brothel operators treated as licensing costs. For example, in Little Rock, brothels were fined $25 per month and $5 per girl, plus $50 per month to sell beer. In Minneapolis, the fine was $50 per month and $5 or $10 for each girl; when reformers there tried to control prostitution in 1897 by doubling the fine, the police started collecting fines every other month.[121]

Some vice districts were famous nationwide, such as Chicago's Levee, New Orleans' Storyville, and San Francisco's Barbary Coast. Prostitution was tolerated in these red light districts, where families and decent women never went. In western towns settled by cowboys and miners – by men working in industry rather than by families – the dance-hall/brothel was one of the most prominent buildings on Main Street.

In Victorian times, most young men were initiated into sex by prostitutes, but women were expected to remain pure until marriage, and the word prostitute could not even be mentioned in mixed company. Thackeray was discrete enough not to mention the word when he talked about how common the practice was:

> ..the ladies were of the rank of those with whom Young Marlow in the comedy is represented as having been familiar before he became abashed in the presence of Miss Hardcastle. The times are such that one scarcely dares to allude to that kind of company, which thousands of our young men ... are frequenting every day, which nightly fills casinos and dancing rooms, which is known to exist as well in the Ring in Hyde Park or the Congregation at St. James's, but which the most squeamish if not the most moral of societies is determined to ignore.[122]

New York was the leading center of the market economy in America, and prostitution was already well established there in the 1830s, with the help of a corrupt police force. It was brought to widespread public notice in 1836, when the madam at a Manhattan brothel checked one of the bedrooms and discovered that a prostitute had apparently been killed by her last customer, Richard Robinson, a nineteen-year old from a good Connecticut family. The "penny press," which had come into existence only three years earlier, carried full transcripts of the three-month-long trial: Robinson claimed that he had been framed by corrupt policemen who were paid off by a dishonest madam, and he was acquitted, possibly because the jury had been bribed.

The invention of the "penny press" during the 1830s was itself a symptom of the Victorian commercialization of sex. After this killing, newspapers printed lithographs of young Robinson fleeing the room and leaving the dead prostitute on her bed, thrilling readers by giving them "a glimpse into the world of illicit sex and the dissolute life of men like Robinson, one of the thousands of single clerks who came into New York for employment, lived in boarding houses, and pursued a life of pleasure in their spare time."[123] This was how men lived when they were not in families.

By the 1830s, also, Tammany Hall was well established in New York as a corrupt Democratic Party machine run by bosses and based on buying support through patronage.[124] The Republican party also had urban political machines during the nineteenth century: The Grant administration was notoriously corrupt, and Grant's supporter Roscoe Conkling ran the Republican political machine in New York city by controlling patronage at New York's custom house. After the Civil War, captains of industry routinely bought favors from Republican congressmen and presidents; the Central Pacific Railroad alone spent $500,000 annually on bribes between 1875 and 1885.[125] In fact, when Benjamin Harrison was elected President in 1888, he was surprised to find that he could not name any members of his own cabinet; the party bosses had sold all the cabinet positions to finance his campaign.[126]

Yet the families of these politicians and of the businessmen who bribed them had no idea of what they did at the office – beyond the fact that they were involved in business, in the sort of thing that men do.

The Victorians lived up to both of their philosophies. In the market economy, self-interest and pleasure reigned, but in the family, the theory of natural law still reigned – sometimes in a grotesquely exaggerated form. For example, Victorians believed that it was unnatural for a mother ever to be selfish and that homosexuality was such a shockingly unnatural act that it dared not speak its name.

The term "liberalism" was first used as the opposite of political and theological conservatism during the nineteenth century, and the split in Victorian society is reflected in the immense difference between liberal economics and liberal theology. In economics, liberals believed that people should be free to pursue their self-interest, to maximize their own satisfaction and pleasure. In theology, liberals believed that people should be free to follow their conscience, and they were even more puritanical than conservatives. We can see in Trollope's novel, *Barchester Towers*, that liberal governments appointed somber, conscience-ridden bishops, who disapproved of pleasures that the conservative high church took for granted.

These two faces of Victorian liberalism both had an important effect on politics. Idealism was the basis of abolitionism, feminism, and other liberal social reforms, and self-interest was the basis of liberal economic policy.

Chapter 4
Modernist Liberalism

Victorian society had two faces because it was in the midst of an economic transition. The self-interested side of it reflected the emerging market economy, and the idealistic side reflected what remained of the home economy. The home economy was still important because modernization had not yet gone far enough to replace all the serious work of the family: Cooking, sewing, cleaning, and raising children were hard and essential work, and charity was also the responsibility of the family, church and voluntary associations.

During the twentieth century, as modernization continued, the home economy became less important, and idealism became less important to liberal thought. Moral individualism was central to classical liberalism; moral individualism was as important as self-interested individualism to Victorian liberalism; but moral individualism became peripheral to modern liberalism during the twentieth century.

During the twentieth century, liberals also abandoned free-market economics and began to claim that economic and social planning were necessary because modernization inevitably made society more centralized and more complex. In the nineteenth century, the modern economy had taken over production. In the twentieth century, liberals believed, centralized organizations would dominate the economy even more completely and would also take over the work of educating our children, protecting our health, and helping the poor.

As the technological economy took over all of the significant work of society, liberals adopted a narrow version of the ideal of negative freedom, which can be called "personal freedom." They believed that people have the right to do anything that they (and other "consenting adults") want to do, as long as it does not hurt someone else. This ideal of freedom comes from John Stuart Mill, but Mill had applied it more broadly to personal behavior and to the serious work of the economy. By contrast, modernist liberals believed that, because the economy was dominated by centralized organizations, this ideal of freedom applies only to personal behavior.

Modernist liberalism became mainstream during the 1960s, when the generation that grew up in the affluent technological society of post-war America came of age. In the 1950s, there were still some remnants of Victorian morality in America, and there were also remnants of the idealistic side of Victorian liberalism in American politics. Quakers and other religious pacifists were early opponents of the Vietnam war, and ministers, such as Martin Luther King, led the early civil right movements. By the 1970s, though, the left had turned to a version of modernist liberalism that combined socialists' demands for entitlements with civil libertarians' demands for personal freedom.

During the early 1960s, many people were attracted to liberalism because it was idealistic, working against bigotry and for civil rights, against McCarthyism and for free speech, and so on. But by the early 1970s, many people had come to believe that liberalism was self indulgent, that it focused on sexual gratification and unlimited entitlements,

This failure of the American left led Americans to support Reaganite conservatism during the 1980s.

The Consumer Economy

During the twentieth century, the market displaced production for use almost completely.

The home lost its productive role and instead became a center of consumption. People stopped sewing clothing for their families, as the garment industry developed in New York and provided cheap ready-to-wear clothing. People spent far less time doing their own laundry after they got washing machines and driers. Families stopped entertaining themselves by playing parlor games, reading aloud or playing the piano as they started listening to radio and television programs produced by the entertainment industry.

The family's most important function was diluted, as schools took over much of the responsibility for raising children. The school system took responsibility for younger and younger children in the course of the twentieth century: Kindergarten became popular early in the century, nursery school in mid-century, and day care for toddlers and even infants during the 1970s.

Like families, local communities lost most of their functions during the twentieth century. Bureaucratic organizations run by the federal government took over the functions of local charities. The federal government grew tremendously, making local governments less important. The automobile also broke up community ties: Instead of walking to local stores where they saw their neighbors, Americans began driving to anonymous regional shopping centers.

The market economy became more centralized and more technologically complex as the industrial monopolies of the late nineteenth century grew into the technological corporations of the twentieth century. Scientific management rationalized industrial production, making older shop skills obsolete.

Even high-level decisions about how corporations should be run were often made by professional managers and engineers rather than by the business's owners. Early in the twentieth century, Thorstein Veblen promoted the ideal of technocracy. The owners of corporations were becoming more dependent on production engineers, and Veblen believed that we were moving toward the point where production would be completely rationalized in a centralized economy "managed by competent technicians with an eye single to maximum production of goods and services."[127]

Influenced by technocratic thinking, progressives believed it was inevitable that scientific planning would ultimately manage every aspect of society. Production engineers would manage the economy. Progressive educators would use the science of psychology to raise children more effectively. City planners would use modern technology to design more livable neighborhoods. These things used to be the responsibility of individuals, families and local governments, but in a modern economy, they would be managed by experts.

Two Sets of Rights

Modernists believed that all of society's serious work would be taken over by big industry and big government, which were too large and impersonal for ordinary people to influence, and which made decisions based on technical questions that ordinary people could not even understand.

The idea of positive freedom – of freedom as the right to run your own business affairs, raise your own children, and help govern your own community – was totally obsolete. Instead, the modernist left focused on two different sets of rights: On the one hand, there was the right to have the technological economy provide you with necessities, and on the other hand, there was the right to a purely negative "personal freedom," freedom from interference when you make private decisions that affect only yourself.

The first set of rights came from nineteenth-century socialism. The second came from nineteenth-century bohemianism. Around the turn of the twentieth century, radical thinkers began to fuse the two to create bohemian socialism.

Oscar Wilde's 1891 essay, "The Soul of Man under Socialism," was the first manifesto of bohemian socialism. Wilde argued that scientific and technological progress would eliminate poverty and drudgery. Because the economy would be collectively owned and managed by the state, progress would also free us from the responsibility of managing our own property. Under socialism – that is, under a fully modernized, state managed economy – people would be freed from all economic constraints and responsibilities, and they would devote themselves entirely to pleasure and to self-expression.[128]

In America, this new political ideal was spread by the bohemian socialists who thrived in Greenwich Village before World War I: The best known were John Reed and Max Eastman, the editors of *The Masses*. This new breed of radical combined the usual socialist demands that the economy should be managed to provide for everyone's needs, with a new set of demands for personal freedoms, such as sexual freedom and the right of women to drink and smoke. Reed and Eastman read Nietzsche, Freud, and D. H. Lawrence, and they believed in will, instinct, and sensuality, like the other rebels against respectability who filled Greenwich Village at the time – and they also believed in science, technology and progress. For example, Eastman said "Lust is divine,"[129] but he also was sure that scientists and engineers, rather than poets and artists, would change society.[130]

Bohemian socialists were very different from nineteenth-century socialists, who believed that people should have the right to necessities and should also have an obligation to work to produce these necessities. Old-fashioned socialists expected that the communist state would draft people into the workforce and assign them to their posts, running the economy like the army. For example, the *Communist Manifesto* talks about "Equal liability of all to labor. Establishment of industrial armies."[131] The principle was: from everyone according to his abilities, to everyone according to his needs – with the state making the decisions about what you need and what work your abilities suit you to contribute.

Nineteenth-century socialism is not part of the history of liberalism: Marx had nothing but scorn for "bourgeois freedoms," such as freedom of speech, freedom of religion, and the freedom to manage your business affairs for yourself. But twentieth-century bohemian socialists anticipated modernist liberalism by combining the socialist idea that people have a right to necessities with the laissez-faire idea that people have a right to behave in any way they please, as long as they do not hurt someone else.

The realm of freedom had become narrower. Laissez-faire liberals expected people to manage their own business affairs, but modernists expected that the technological economy would take over all the serious work and planners would make the economic decisions. In a modern technological society, there was room for freedom only in the realm of purely personal behavior.

Modernism Becomes Mainstream

Bohemian socialism disappeared after World War I, when socialists began look to Russia for their ideology, but its two ideals – the planned technological economy and personal freedom – became major themes of twentieth-century culture.

We can see these two ideals in the avant garde art of the twentieth century. Modernist architecture was dominated by functionalism, a school that wanted to design buildings, cities, and entire societies as purely rational expressions of technology. And modernist painting was dominated by dada, surrealism, and abstract expressionism, schools that wanted to throw away inhibitions and let repressed content well up from the unconscious. The austerity of modernist architecture is so different from the wild self-expression of modernist painting because architects worked in the public realm, with its ideal of technological planning, while painters explored the private realm, with its ideal of personal freedom.

As its name implied, the avant garde was an advance force leading the rest of society into modernity. In the course of the twentieth century, its radical ideals gradually entered the liberal mainstream.

The radicals' ideal in personal freedom began to enter the mainstream during the 1920s – with the rejection of Victorian restraints, the partial sexual freedom, and the heavy drinking that were typical of the jazz age. In a complete turn-about from the nineteenth century, liberals began to attack Puritanism: Nineteenth-century liberals had thought that, though they were narrow and dogmatic, the Puritans began the reform movement that they themselves were working to complete,[132] but during the twentieth century, liberals began to think the Puritans represented the "repression" that they were fighting against.

The radicals' belief in technological planning began to enter the mainstream early in the twentieth century, during the progressive era. Some of the progressives' ideas were technocratic: For example, they introduced the city manager form of government and civil service exams, to replace corrupt urban political machines with professional experts. But the progressives combined this economic modernism with social conservatism, and they looked for ways to preserve older American ideals in modern times: For example, they introduced initiative, referendum, and recall as modern extensions of the ideal of democracy.

Liberals became true believers in technological planning during the 1930s, when the Great Depression convinced Americans that they were dependent on an economic machine that they could not understand or control. The New Deal brought technocratic ideas into the liberal mainstream – among Roosevelt's advisors, Rexford Tugwell and Stuart Chase were followers of Veblen – but most liberals differed from Veblen because they thought that corporate management could help do the planning. Liberal economists claimed that, because the modern corporation had become too complex for its owners to manage, our largest private corporations were managed by analysts, engineers, and administrators, who aimed to promote stability and economic growth rather than to maximize owners' profits.[133] As Keynes put it, modern industry tended to "socialize itself."[134] Liberals wanted big government to work with big business to promote stability; the government would manage the economy to prevent recessions and would promote growth by building power projects, highways, and dams.

Ordinary people were totally dependent on this corporate-state economy. During the Depression, when the economy faltered and people were unemployed and destitute through no fault of their own, the socialist idea that there is a right to be provided with necessities seemed compelling. Roosevelt incorporated it into the liberal creed when he gave his famous speech about the "four freedoms": freedom of speech, freedom of religion, freedom from want, and freedom from fear. The first two freedoms came from the Bill of Rights, and the second two freedoms gave Americans a new right to be taken care of.

Post-War America

Because our economy thrived during World War II, while the rest of the world was ravaged, post-war America was the first place where modernization reached its logical conclusion, a technological consumer society.

Industry was oligopolistic – for example, there were three automobile manufacturers, and General Motors was the "price leader" that set prices for the entire industry – and according to liberal economists such as John Kenneth Galbraith, these giant corporations were run not by their owners but by expert managers whose goal was to insure stability and maximize economic growth.[135] Keynesian economists in Washington managed the economy as a whole to insure stability and growth. Other federal planners built the public works, such as freeways, that were needed to accommodate growth. There were gaps in the technological economy, which liberals wanted new federal planning organizations to fill – for example, liberals wanted the federal government to clear slums and build low-income housing – but on the whole, the corporate-state economy was working and was providing everyone with a rising standard of living.

According to Galbraith and some other liberals, large corporations were able to generate enough retained earnings to fund their own investments, so there was no longer any need for ordinary people to save. Instead, people had the new economic role of consumers: "The individual serves the industrial system not by supplying it with savings and the resulting capital; he serves it by consuming its products."[136] The educational system was turning out more skilled workers than ever, but factories were so productive that wages were high even for unskilled labor. It seemed that you no longer needed to learn a skill to join the middle-class: Even factory workers could afford a house in one of the suburban subdivision that developers were building all over the country and a car to drive on the freeways that the government was building all over the country.

In the new suburban homes, families gathered around the television. Frozen meals became a popular substitute for cooking, and they were called "TV Dinners" – implying that people are better off if they can eat dinner without taking any time off from being entertained. Suburbanites talked about family "togetherness," but they meant that parents should be friends and companions of their children; the main responsibility for raising children was passed to the schools, the nursery schools, and, if all else failed, the child psychologists.

Social critics called post-war America a "consumer society" not just because people were affluent enough to consume more than ever before, but also because people thought of themselves as consumers whose needs had to be fulfilled for them by the economic system. Virtually everyone believed that, in a modern society, the centralized economy had to provide us with housing, transportation, education, and jobs, and that expert managers had to run the centralized economy – and the entire society. As John F. Kennedy said:

> Most of us are conditioned for many years to have a political viewpoint – Republican or Democratic, liberal, conservative or moderate. The fact of the matter is that most of the problems ... that we now face are technical problems, are administrative problems. They are very sophisticated judgments, questions which are now beyond the comprehension of most men.[137]

The Sixties

During the economic boom of the 1960s, this vision of the modern economy seemed triumphant. Many people believed that Keynesian planners had learned to control the business cycle and promote endless growth, without recessions. Affluence was widespread.

Modernist liberalism reached its high point at the same time. Liberals of the 1960s carried technological optimism to an extreme. People were in the habit of saying, "If they can put a man on the moon, why can't they..." rebuild the slums, keep traffic flowing, educate every child, and so on. Every social question was a problem that could be solved by mobilizing money and expertise, like the technological problem of putting a man on the moon.

The federal government was supposed to use the same technological approach to eliminate poverty. It would clear slums, build model housing projects, provide jobs for the poor, and provide any remaining unemployed with income that would keep them above the poverty line. At the time, liberals used to say that we could abolish poverty "with the stroke of a pen," if the president just signed a law guaranteeing everyone an adequate income.

Classical Jeffersonian liberals wanted to preserve an economy based on small property and an independent civil society. Laissez-faire liberals believed in the free market, and they refused to admit that it threatened small property and civil society. Modernist liberals took it for granted that the modern corporation and state were replacing small property and civil society, and they wanted government to give people a bigger piece of the pie.

The modernist ideal of personal freedom spread through America during the 1960s and 1970s, along with the modernist idea that technology could do everything.

Among 1960s radicals, there was a revival of bohemian socialism. Students for a Democratic Society and other radical groups combined the old socialist demands for more government funded health care, education, and jobs, with the new culture of sex, drugs and rock and roll.

Liberals adopted a more moderate form of bohemian socialism. By the late 1960s, liberals believed in government programs to provide everyone with housing, health care, education, and jobs, and they also believed in tolerance for "alternative lifestyles."

The word "lifestyle" became popular during the 1960s and 1970s, as Americans focused on the self with some of the same earnestness that Victorians felt about their families: People talked endlessly about getting in touch with your own feelings, exploring your own consciousness, finding your own identity, defining your own lifestyle, choosing your own values. Powerless to act in the public world, people turned inward – to psychotherapy, drugs and meditation or to piercing their bodies and dying their hair purple – asserting their individuality in the only realm where they still had any freedom.

The perfect symbol of the sixties is a Mies van der Rohe office building with Jackson Pollack paintings in its lobby. The technological system produces a perfectly engineered building, and the people in it express themselves through uninhibited action. Both of these styles began early in the twentieth century, as avant garde art that was meant as a radical attack on traditional society. But by the 1960s, the most prestigious new corporate high-rises were built in these styles: The avant garde began to look less radical and more like the status quo of the technological society.

Modernist Philosophy

In the twentieth century, most philosophers believed that reason is purely instrumental: Reason can tell us the best way to reach a goal, but it cannot tell us whether the goal itself is good. Idealism and natural law philosophy, which believed that reason could tell us which goals are good and which are bad, were displaced by scientific empiricism and praxis philosophy,[138] which believe that our "values" are subjective.

This moral relativism became central to modernist liberalism.

Positivism and Pragmatism

In the early to mid twentieth century, the two philosophies that were most important to American liberalism were positivism and pragmatism. Both reflected the great prestige that scientific knowledge rightfully had at the time, and both mistakenly devalued other forms of knowledge. These two philosophies believed that the ideas that ordinary people had about what sort of lives they wanted to live did not have the same ontological value as the ideas of scientists and planners, so both made it more difficult for ordinary people to use technology for human purposes.

Positivism

Positivism was empiricist, but it rejected the attempt to make empiricism the basis of ethics. Nineteenth-century utilitarianism tried to base ethics on our experience that pleasure is good and pain is bad. Positivism, by contrast, said that experience could give us knowledge about what is, but it could not give us knowledge about what should be.

Logical positivism claimed that that only two types of sciences are valid: Empirical sciences such as physics can tell us what exists in the world, and formal sciences such as mathematics can develop logical tools that help analyze the world. Ethics does not involve either of these forms of knowledge, so it was considered nothing more than subjective "value judgments" that are statements about personal likes or dislikes. One logical positivist summed it up by saying that moral terms – words such as "good" and "bad" or "right" and "wrong" – are really just "purr words" and "growl words" that express our emotional reaction to something we like or dislike.[139]

The logical positivists were reacting against Hegel's philosophy, which had been used to justify state power in

German speaking countries. Hegelian idealists claimed to be talking scientifically about moral truths, and the logical positivists attacked them by saying that all "value judgments" are just statements about the feelings of the people who make them.

Karl Popper's book *The Open Society and its Enemies*, was one of the most important attacks on totalitarianism in post-war America, and it made positivism an important liberal philosophy of that time.[140] Popper traced the history of authoritarianism from Plato to Hegel to Marx, whom he criticized for being "essentialists," who believed there was such a thing as human nature. Though Marx called himself a materialist and an atheist, Popper claimed he was primarily a mystic:

> [Marx] misled scores of intelligent people into believing that historical prophesy is the scientific way of approaching social problems.... The fact that Russia is making bold and often successful experiments in social engineering has led many to infer that Marxism, as the science or creed which underlies the Russian experiment, must be a kind of social technology, or at least favorable to it. But nobody who knows anything about the history of Marxism can make this mistake. Marxism is a purely historical theory.... As such, it certainly did not furnish the basis of the policy of the Russian Communist Party after its rise to political power. Since Marx had practically forbidden all social technology, which he denounced as Utopian, his Russian disciples found themselves at first entirely unprepared for their great tasks in the field of social engineering.[141]

Popper was a great believer in social engineering: "The social engineer believes that a scientific basis of politics would ... consist of the factual information necessary for the construction or alteration of social institutions...."[142]

Popper said that social engineers were concerned with finding the best means to a given end, rather than with the ends themselves.[143] He believed that philosophers had always been wrong to talk about the "normative laws" that define these ends as if they were the same as the natural laws discovered by science: these moral laws were actually social conventions with no basis in nature.[144] Rather than "utopian social engineering," which sets larger human goals for the social engineers, Popper believed in "piecemeal social engineering," which lets the engineers deal with social problems as they come up, because piecemeal social engineering could be experimental and critical, learning from its errors.[145]

In post-war America, Popper was obviously aiming at the wrong targets. At the beginning of the century, positivism challenged the power of the Kaiser or of the Austro-Hungarian Emperor by encouraging critical thought. But Popper was helping to legitimize the most important new form of power in modern America – the power of expert decision-makers, from economic planners to traffic engineers to educational psychologists. These planners make objectively valid decisions by gathering and analyzing empirical data, while ordinary people's opinions about the goals that technology should be used for – about what the economy should produce, what sort of cities they should live in, or how their children should be raised – are merely "value judgments," merely statements about their own feelings.

Pragmatism

Positivism believed only in the truths of science. John Dewey's pragmatism, the other major liberal philosophy of the early to mid twentieth century, redefined truth so the scientific method could apply to politics and ethics as well as to science.

Pragmatists rejected the usual metaphysical arguments of philosophers who tried to show that our ways of knowing things are adequate to understand the way that the universe actually is. Instead, they said that our mind evolved because it is useful to manipulate ideas, just as our hands evolved because they are useful to manipulate objects. An idea is true if it is useful and successful in manipulating the world; we should ignore the old correspondence theory of truth, which asks whether our statements are objectively true because they describe the world accurately, and replace it with a progmatist theory of truth which says ideas are true if they are useful.

Like Popper, Dewey disliked Marxist ideology but believed that the world needed organized economic planning like the planning that was done in Russia.

> I cannot obtain intellectual, moral or esthetic satisfaction from the professed philosophy which animates Bolshevik Russia. But I am sure that the future historian of our times will ... [admire] those who had the imagination first to see that the resources of technology might be directed by organized planning to serve chosen ends....[146]

We cannot resist the shift toward a more centralized, corporate economy: "Economic determinism is now a fact, not a theory. But there is a difference and a choice between a blind, chaotic and unplanned determinism, issuing from business conducted for pecuniary profit, and the determinism of a socially planned and ordered development.[147]

Like Popper, Dewey was a believer in social engineering, and he hoped that centralized planning would bring "a real application of the engineering mind to social life in its economic phase."[148]

Unlike Popper, Dewey redefined ethics as the application of the engineering mentality to social problems. In his book *Reconstruction in Philosophy*, Dewey sketched what philosophy would be like if it abandoned the old metaphysical approach, that grew out of the ancient Greeks' aristocratic disdain for manual labor, in favor of a pragmatist approach that grows out of our society's economic dynamism.

Its chapter on ethics criticizes the Greeks for trying to replace traditional morality with morality based on reasoning about the good life: "reason as a substitute for custom was under the obligation of supplying objects and laws as fixed as those of custom had been."[149] Dewey rejects these fixed ends, arguing that "Moral goods and ends exist only when something has to be done,"[150] so ethics should be redefined as practical work to solve problems:

> ...experimental logic when carried into morals makes every quality that is judged to be good according as it contributes to amelioration of existing ills. ... When physics, chemistry, biology, medicine, contribute to the detection of concrete human woes and to the development of plans for remedying them, they become moral; they become part of the apparatus of moral inquiry of science. ... Natural science ... becomes in itself humanistic in quality. It is something to be pursued not in a technical and

specialized way for what is called truth for its own sake, but with the sense of its social bearing. ... It is technical only in the sense that it provides the technique of social and moral engineering.[151]

It seems that Dewey has replaced religious faith with an equally profound faith in technology and progress, which he considers good in itself, saying, "the process of growth, improvement and progress, rather than the static outcome and result, become the significant thing. ... Growth itself is the only moral 'end.'"[152]

Dewey wanted to revive the sense of community that people have when they work together, but as a pragmatist, he did not believe that the community could base decisions on its ideas about the good life.

He thought that ideas were tools we use to manipulate the world, and that people are indulging in meaningless metaphysics when they ask what is the good life.

For pragmatists, reason can tell you the best way to reach a goal, but it cannot criticize the goal itself. In this view, reason can never tell you that it is time to limit growth on moral and political grounds, because you have enough. This view implies that engineers and planners have good rational grounds for their decisions about how to use technology, but ordinary people cannot decide how they want to use technology based on their ideas about how they want to live.

In America of the 1950s and 1960s, many liberals called themselves "pragmatists." They said we had reached "the end of ideology."[153] Instead of engaging in the old ideological debates about what is a good society, we would act practically by mobilizing money and expertise to solve social problems. We would spend money on freeways planned by transportation engineers to solve our traffic problems. We would use federal deficit spending planned by Keynesian economists to promote economic growth and solve our unemployment problems. We would not waste our time on ideological debates about the goals of these policies – about whether we would be a better society if we built walkable neighborhoods where people drive less or if we worked shorter hours so we had more time but slower economic growth.

Postmodernism and Multiculturalism

After the 1960s, the American left – both radicals and liberals – moved beyond pragmatism to more extreme versions of praxis philosophy, which hold that ideas are nothing more than instruments of power, of desire, or of will. Dewey said that idea are true if they are useful in manipulating the world, and the praxis philosophers go further by saying that ideas are not true or false; they are merely byproducts of action. Popularized by the radicals of the 1960s and 1970s, this view was the basis of postmodernism and multiculturalism, which became the conventional wisdom of liberals in American colleges and universities of the later twentieth century.

Influences on Postmodernism

Postmodernists are influenced by Freud, Marx and Nietzsche, the thinkers who did the most to debunk nineteenth century idealism. These three thinkers all anticipate praxis philosophy.

Freudians said that religious or philosophical ideas are merely sublimated expressions of our instincts. Rather than talking about whether ideas are true or false, they search for the instinctual drives and infantile experiences behind them. But they apply this principle to everyone except themselves: They believe Freudian psychoanalysis is an objective science. In reality, it should be obvious by now that Freudianism was more a cultural movement than a science, expressing the repressed impulses that were welling up as the modern economy eroded Victorian morality, as surrealist art did. Its theories have never been confirmed empirically and generally accepted, like the theories of the hard sciences.[154]

Marxists said that that our ideas are merely expressions of economic interests – an ideological superstructure set up to justify class interests. Rather than talking about whether ideas are true or false, they search for the economic interests behind them. When people deviate from the party line, they accuse them of "false consciousness" or of being "objectively on the side of the bourgeoisie"; they do not say that the deviant ideas are untrue but that they do not reflect the interest of the working class. Most Marxists fall into the same sort of self-contradiction as the Freudians by making only one exception to their ideological analysis of ideas: They believe Marxism is an objectively true science.

Marx himself sometimes went further. Because he was a real philosopher, he sometimes moved toward pure praxis philosophy and said that socialist ideas themselves were an expression of working class interests, that they were true only in the sense that they would be successful historically. In *The German Ideology*, he ridiculed "true socialists,"[155] who considered socialism an ideal that society should conform to, and who criticized the working class when it departs from their idea of "true socialism." In reality, Marx says, socialism is the working class ideology that is actually effective in history, so it is meaningless to criticize the working class for deviating from true socialism. Here Marx implies that socialist ideas are true only in the sense that they will make the working class the dominant class, but Marx never discussed this pragmatist theory of truth explicitly, and he contradicted it in later books that claimed to analyze history scientifically.

The purest praxis philosophy comes from Nietzsche, who believed that all ideals were merely an expression of the will to power. Nietzsche said we adopt ideas not because of their "truth value" but because of their "life value," and that we can never get beyond the practical life value of ideas to find whether there is any truth behind them. He said that "There are no facts, only interpretations," and he rejected the philosophical search for truth in favor of "perspectivism": Rather than arguing that ideas were true or false, as philosophers had done in the past, we should increase our understanding of a subject by looking at from many different viewpoints.

Nietzsche rejected transcendent ideals as well as transcendent knowledge. His central project was the "transvaluation of values," replacing the "slave values" of Socrates and Christianity, which foster weakness, with values that would release human vitality. He set out to destroy traditional philosophical and religious ideals, which the weakling masses had created to control the vitality of the aristocracy.

Postmodernism

During the 1960s, Marx and Freud were the favorites, but during the 1970s, Nietzsche became the favorite of radical postmodernists, who used Nietzsche's perspectivism to claim that all ideas and ideals are social constructs that limit our freedom by making us conform to society's system of power.

Jacques Derrida believed that we can increase freedom by deconstructing texts, destroying their claim to truth, which is just an attempt to assert power. Deconstructionists tried to expand freedom by attacking "essentialism," the idea that there is any human nature, but they also went much further by attacking the ideas of truth and meaning. As one deconstructionist said (in the usual prose style), "The whole ideology of representational signification is an ideology of power. To break its spell, we would have to attack writing, totalistic representational signification...."[156] A graduate student put it more succinctly when he said "meaning is fascist."[157]

Michel Foucault, following Nietzsche, tried to show that norms of behavior are nothing more than categories imposed on us by power. He argued that the ideas of crime and even of madness[158] are arbitrary social constructs that serve the interests of those in power. This was a popular theory during the 1960s, when it was sometimes called "labeling theory"[159] – the idea that we consider behavior deviant only because society labels it as deviant.

Postmodernism is very much in the modernist tradition. According to Jean-Francois Lyotard, one of its most influential theorists, postmodernism began when artists realized that the old avant garde works were no longer new and shocking, that artists had to go in new directions in order to continue breaking with tradition as shockingly as avant garde modernists had.[160] But for all their straining after novelty, they have not moved beyond the attempt to break through boundaries to personal freedom that was the fundamental idea of modernism a century ago, at the time of the dadaists. One deconstructionist summed it up when he called himself a "Derridadaist."

Multiculturalism

Postmodernists spread their ideas most successfully by promoting multiculturalism in the schools. They followed

Neitzsche's perspectivism, claiming that diversity itself improves education by bringing new perspectives to the universities: The classics just represent a white male perspective, and it is also valuable to have a black perspective, a woman's perspective, a gay perspective, and so on. Ideas are just expressions of power, and it follows that the classics are not works that stand out because of their excellence; they have been imposed on everyone because white males have power. Ethnic groups and other subgroups (such as women, gays and lesbians) should study their own cultures, which are just as valid as white male culture.

Multiculturalists are relativists because they hope to promote tolerance and equality, but their relativism can also be used to justify fascism. If all cultures are equally valid, if all cultures are just assertions of power, than there are no objective moral standards to stop one ethnic group from asserting its power by eliminating other ethnic groups. Hatred of Jews was an important part of German culture beginning in the middle ages, when the Jews were expelled from Germany because they were considered to be the cause of bubonic plague. If we condemn the Nazis for slaughtering the Jews, we are just imposing our values on another culture: We are condemning the Nazis because they did not agree with the narrow American perspective that all people have the inalienable right to life.[161]

In addition, this new moral relativism could not allow us to develop a common idea of the good life, any more than positivism or pragmatism could. At the very time when we needed to revive the classical idea of the good life to allow us to use technology for human purposes, liberals promoted moral relativism that made it impossible even to discuss the good life.

From Idealism to Modernism

American liberals abandoned idealism for modernism during the 1960s. Victorian values still had some influence in America in the 1950s, and the idealism of classical and Victorian liberalism also still had influence at the time. But the nation rejected Victorian values during the 1960s, and it rejected classical liberalism at the same time.

Because of this sudden change, the public perception of liberalism changed dramatically during the 1960s and 1970s. Liberalism had been considered idealistic in 1960, but it seemed self-indulgent by 1970.

The Civil Rights Movement

The change was very dramatic in the civil rights movement, because this movement began in the south, an economically backward part of the country where modernization had not gone far enough to undermine classical liberalism, and then moved to the cities of the north, the part of the country where modernization had gone the furthest.

Classical liberal ideals were still strong when the civil rights movement began in the south of the 1950s. As Christopher Lasch has shown, Martin Luther King built his movement in the south on the churches, the stable families and the small businesses of the black community, he encouraged communities to organize cooperative credit unions, finance companies, and grocery stores to develop self-reliance, and he reminded his followers that "We must not let the fact that we are the victims of injustice lull us into abrogating responsibility for our own lives."[162]

King was the last great figure in the long tradition of liberal idealism. Like many nineteenth century abolitionists and feminists, he based his movement on Christian natural law theory. He defended civil disobedience on these grounds in his famous "Letter from a Birmingham Jail":

> One has not only a legal but a moral responsibility to obey just laws. Conversely, one has a moral responsibility to disobey unjust laws. ... A just law is a man-made code that squares with the moral law or the law of God. An unjust law is a code that is out of harmony with the moral law. To put it in the terms of St. Thomas Aquinas: An unjust law is a human law that is not rooted in eternal law and natural law.[163]

King attacked racism by appealing to universal moral standards: As he said in his famous "I have a dream" speech, people should "not be judged by the color of their skin, but by the content of their character." People are equal in the sense that the same moral standards apply to us all, regardless of race.

He also called not only for non-violence but for love of those who persecute you. The early Civil Rights movement was so attractive – particularly to the idealistic young – because it criticized the standards of society by invoking higher moral standards.

By the late 1960s, though, the movement for racial equality had shifted to the urban north, the most thoroughly modernized part of the country, where civil society, the family and self-reliance had broken down much more drastically than they had in small towns of the south. As Lasch shows, it was only after he moved north that King began to talk about socialism[164] – demanding services for people, rather than removing barriers to people's own efforts – and he was joined by local leaders who had always thought this way.

When it moved to the North, the civil rights movement veered suddenly from classical, moral liberalism to modernist liberalism, with its demands that the government provide services, and with a moral relativism that hurt African Americans even more than other Americans, because their poverty made them more vulnerable.

The most extreme northern civil rights leaders in the north began to argue that blacks were equal to whites not because all people should be held to the same moral standards, as King had said, but because all standards were imposed by those in power, as Neitzsche had said – and anyone who believed in objective standards was a racist.

The most dramatic example of this moral relativism was the outraged reaction to the 1965 Moynihan report on the black family, which said that the rising number of births to unwed mothers – accounting for about 25% of black children when Moynihan wrote – was a threat to the well-being of African Americans. Liberals shouted that the black "matriarchal family" was an adaptation to historical circumstances, which was just as valid for blacks as the "nuclear family" was for whites, and that Moynihan was a racist. The indignation was so overwhelming that, as William J. Wilson says, social scientists were not willing to study the black family again for more than a decade, because they were afraid of being called racists.[165]

When academics began to study the black family again, the relativists lost the debate, because family breakdown had become so obviously destructive that the damage could no longer be ignored: Today, over two-thirds of African-American children are born to unwed mothers.

The Failure of Modernist Liberalism

If people believe they have a right to choose any personal behavior or "lifestyle," and that their problems are the fault of "the system," the result will obviously be social decline. During the 1960s and 1970s, when modernist liberalism was at its most influential, educational achievement, measured by SAT scores and other standardized tests, fell dramatically; though scores improved during the 1980s and 1990s, and they still not back to their 1963 peak. The crime rate soared during the 1960s and 1970s, increasing almost five-fold before it began falling during the 1990s. Births to unwed mothers rose from 6% of all births in 1960 to about 40% of all births in America today.

Modernist liberalism collapsed. In the 1970s and 1980s, many academics and writers who had been liberal became neo-conservatives, because they were appalled by the results that modernist liberalism had in practice. Reagan's victory in 1980 represented a shift to the right that led most liberals to abandon moral relativism.

One of the last modernist liberals in government was Joycelyn Elders, President Clinton's first Surgeon General: When she was asked by a reporter whether it was right to have children out of wedlock, she answered, "Everyone has different moral standards.... You can't impose your standards on someone else."[166] Clinton dismissed her because he was embarrassed by her views, though liberals had all united behind this same idea when the Moynihan report came out in 1965.

The idealism of the early civil rights movement in the South, the fact that it upheld moral standards higher than the standards of society as a whole, was one reason that American liberalism was so attractive during the early

1960s. The moral decline that occurred after the movement shifted north and turned modernist, focusing on entitlements and personal freedom, was one cause of the decline of liberalism that begin in the 1970s. Conservatives pointed at the breakdown of the family and the rise of a welfare dependent underclass to show how badly liberalism had failed.

Chapter 5
Personal Freedom in the Courts

Liberal thinking about civil liberties also shifted suddenly from idealism to modernism during the 1960s, at about the same time as liberal thinking about racial equality. Before 1960, for example, the American Civil Liberties Union concentrated on defending political speech and serious literary and scientific speech, such as the right to teach evolution – cases where freedom of speech is based on the obligation to say what we believe is true.[167] Beginning in the 1960s, the ACLU continued to defend these sorts of serious speech on the rare occasions when they were threatened – for example, when the ACLU defended the right of the Nazis to assemble and speak in Skokie, Illinois, in 1978 – but the defense of pornography became the main focus of their work on free speech.

They shifted from the classical to the modernist idea of civil liberties. Instead of defending public acts, they began defending private acts: Political, literary and scientific speech are meant to convince the public, but pornography is used for private pleasure. Instead of defending people acting out of a sense of obligation, they began defending people seeking self-gratification.

Classical liberalism protected the right to act publicly. Freedom of speech is meaningless unless you are speaking to other people. Freedom of assembly is meaningless unless you are assembling with other people. Freedom of religion allowed groups of people to create a key institution of civil society, rather than being forced into the established church. Families and small businesses were to be free from arbitrary interference because they are the foundation of civil society. All these rights involve positive freedom to act in the public world.

By contrast, laissez-faire and modernist liberalism defend private actions. Society is a collection of self-interested individuals, who have the right to do what they please as long as they do not harm other individuals. Rights draw lines between people so no one interferes with someone else's private actions. Rather than protecting the positive freedom to act publicly, rights protect negative freedom, freedom from any interference in your own private sphere.

During the twentieth century, modernization went far enough that liberals came to think of society as nothing but individuals and impersonal technological organizations. Modernist liberals defended the personal freedom of the individuals – their right to act in ways that affect only themselves and other consenting adults – and they expected the technological organizations to take care of them.

In some cases, the modernists' defense of personal freedom has led to real legal advances. For example, the Supreme Court first established the right to privacy in *Griswold v. Connecticut* (1965), which gave married couples the right to use birth control. Today, it seems astounding that just a half century ago, the state of Connecticut – of all places – wanted to control its citizens' behavior in their own bedrooms by making it illegal for married couples to use birth control. Despite the tortured reasoning of the court in this case, which found the right to privacy lurking in the "penumbras" of other constitutional rights, there is no doubt that there was a need for this new right during the twentieth century, as modern technology was giving the government new ways to invade citizens' privacy. The founders did not foresee a world where you would have to worry that Big Brother is watching you, so they did not talk explicitly about the right to privacy, but the Fourth Amendment did establish the "right of the people to be secure in their persons, houses, papers, and effects, against unreasonable searches and seizures," showing that the founders were concerned with protecting the private realm from the threats to it that existed at the time they wrote.

Though the modernist liberals' work for personal freedom did have value in some cases, this chapter will look at the limitations of modernist liberalism by considering court decisions where liberals thought that they were expanding freedom by protecting narrowly personal actions but instead were emptying freedom of content. The First Amendment rights to freedom of religion, freedom of assembly, and freedom of speech were meant to protect the freedom to act in the public realm, but modernist liberals reinterpreted them so to protect personal freedom, to protect private actions that affect only the individual. They carried negative freedom further than ever before, but they applied it to a private realm that was narrower than ever before – a realm so narrow that it leaves little room to do anything significant.

Religion as Personal Behavior

The First Amendment says, "Congress shall make no law respecting an establishment of religion, or prohibiting the free exercise thereof." Modernist liberals privatized freedom of religion by interpreting the Establishment

==clause to keep religion out of the public realm, saying that the First Amendment requires "separation of church and state" so that religious activity cannot be allowed in public places and cannot receive government funding.==

In *Everson v. Board of Education* (1947), a suit sponsored by the ACLU, the Court upheld a program providing bus transportation to private and public school students but also said for the first time that the First Amendment creates a "wall of separation" between church and state.[168] This ambiguous decision energized both sides in the battle over separation of church and state: A coalition of the ACLU and two liberal religious groups fought a series of court battles to remove religion from public life.

In some cases, these separationists were attacking compulsory public religious observances that really were violations of freedom of conscience. For example, in *Engel v. Vitale* (1962), the Court found that it was unconstitutional for the New York public schools to require student prayer.

In other cases, the separationists were fighting to remove religion from public life entirely, to limit people to practicing their religions in private. For example, the ACLU filed suit annually to stop religious displays on public property.[169] The ACLU also sued to stop voluntary student religious groups from using school building for after school meetings, even if any other voluntary student group may use the building for meetings. And the ACLU has fought a long battle, beginning with *Everson*, against government aid to religious schools, even when the aid does not serve any religious purpose and is given equally to all schools, religious and non-religious.

In all these cases, the "wall of separation" is not being used to stop compulsory religious exercises, such as school prayer, which do involve a sort of establishment of religion. Instead, it is being used to place a special burden on religion. According to the ACLU, the state can aid any private schools – except schools run by religious groups. Students can use a public school meeting room to study any book – except the Bible, the Koran, or the Bhagavad Gita. Any organization can apply to set up a display on public property to promote its beliefs – except a religious organization.[170]

More recently, a conservative Supreme Court rejected the liberals' separationism. For example, it has required that public schools must give equal treatment to accommodate religious and non-religious clubs who want to use their facilities. Most strikingly, a conservative majority ruled in *Zelman v. Simmons-Harris* (2002) that it is constitutional to provide school vouchers that parents can spend in either religious or secular schools, with the four liberal justices dissenting.

This sort of neutrality toward religion was obviously the intention of the First Amendment's Establishment clause. In England at the time of the American revolution, dissenters had to pay taxes to support the Church of England, in addition to the donations they gave to support their own churches. When the founders wrote the First Amendment, they undoubtedly had this extra financial burden for religious dissenters in the back of their mind, because it was the most obvious burden on freedom of religion at the time. Today, there is a similar financial burden for parents who send their children to religious schools, who have to pay taxes to support the public schools in addition to paying for private school, and liberals have defended this burden on religion by arguing against the constitutionality of vouchers that may be used at all private schools, including religious schools.

There is one modern case where the Court protected the serious, public meaning of freedom of religion, *Wisconsin v. Yoder* (1972), which gave the Amish the right not to send their children to High School. As compulsory schooling laws were extended to cover older children, they began to conflict with the Amish religious belief that children should go to elementary school but not to High School, which they believed taught children to be competitive and worldly. In several states in the Midwest, groups of Amish teenagers had to run into cornfields to hide from the police who had come to take them to school. The Amish were driven out of Nebraska entirely by that state's strict enforcement of compulsory education laws: Despite the First Amendment, a state persecuted and eliminated an entire religious community. Yet the ACLU and other liberal civil rights groups did not participate in Wisconsin v. Yoder, which was filed by an *ad hoc* group organized by a Lutheran minister. Modernist liberals did not seem to care about a case where freedom of religion is positive freedom to do something significant – to raise your children in the way you believe is right.

Loitering as Freedom of Assembly

Modernist liberals also privatized freedom of assembly by arguing that anti-loitering laws and curfew laws violate the First Amendment.

In the classical liberal view, freedom of assembly and association protect the positive freedom to hold political meetings and form voluntary organizations. Authoritarian societies, at the time when the founders adopted the First Amendment and throughout history, tried to limit political meetings and voluntary organizations, because they threatened the power of the government and of the established church. In the modernist view, by contrast, these First Amendment rights protect people who are hanging out aimlessly on street corners.

Modernist liberals claimed that anti-loitering laws violate the First Amendment's protection of freedom of assembly, and they prevailed in a few cases, such as Coates v. City of Cincinnati (1971).[171] But the key case that struck down anti-loitering laws, Papachristou v. City of Jacksonville (1972), did so on the grounds that these laws were unconstitutionally vague. Laws typically defined loitering as "standing or walking around aimlessly," and the court found that police ignored middle-class people standing on the street waiting for friends but arrested poor people doing exactly the same thing. This decision made cities pass "loitering plus" laws, which define the crime much more precisely, such as laws against loitering with the intent to sell drugs.[172]

But without the old-fashioned anti-loitering laws that this decision struck down, shopping streets or neighborhood parks can turn into campgrounds for the homeless or into hang-outs for teenagers, who get there when school lets out and stay until after midnight with radios blasting. The people who live in a neighborhood lose control over how its parks and streets are used.

As Americans became less able to control the public realm, they began to move to gated communities, which keep out everyone except the residents. They shop at malls whose streets are private property, because the owners can control who hangs out there – and in most states, the owners of shopping malls can restrict political speech as well as loitering.[173] They have even begun to take young children to private, pay-by-the-hour playgrounds, rather than to public parks.

Instead of anti-loitering laws and curfews for teenagers, modernist liberals want the government to provide after-school programs and summer programs for teenagers. The most notorious example was the federally funded "midnight basketball" program of the 1990s: Cities kept recreational centers open until after midnight on weekends, so teenagers could play basketball there all evening, but the teenagers were required to talk to youth workers about their problems before they were allowed to play. The striking thing about this sort of program is that, despite their talk about liberties, modernists want to keep children and teenagers under almost constant government surveillance – even at midnight – and they want the government's youth workers to pry into the details of their personal lives.

There would be much less government control over the children if we could pass laws that act in a limited way, by banning only behavior that can be destructive, rather than putting children in therapeutic programs that control them full time.

For example, laws banning teenage loitering after dark would be much less intrusive than midnight basketball. Curfew law are expensive to enforce, because teenagers who violate them are taken to the police station and their parents are called to take them home. In addition, curfews usually are not applied before 10 or 11 PM, because people do not want to keep teenagers imprisoned in their homes all evening.[174] By contrast, laws against loitering after dark would not prevent teenagers from going places in the evening, only from hanging out on the streets or in parks. These laws would be easy to enforce: Police could just tell loiterers to move on. They would apply to all teenagers and would not be selectively enforced. They would not control teenagers totally, like the modernists' youth programs and midnight basketball; instead, they would stop behavior that can become self-destructive, so the teenagers would find other things to do on their own.

More general anti-loitering laws are also needed to allow communities to build parks, playgrounds, and other public facilities without worrying that they will be taken over by people who come to hang out all day. These laws could make it illegal to remain in one location in a public park for more than three hours or to remain in one location on the sidewalk for more than half an hour except for specifically defined purposes (such as political leafleting), so they would not be enforced selectively. Without this sort of law, anyone who drifts into town can walk into a park first thing in the morning, spread out his possessions, and stay there all day, every day – which is why neighborhood groups sometimes try to stop new parks that are planned in their neighborhoods.

As Amitai Etzioni has said, people who oppose this sort of law are not really protecting everyone's rights, as they think; they are "radical individualists"[175] who believe the right of any one person to use a public space outweighs the rights of everyone else in the community to use that space. If a community decides to build a playground for children, that decision should not be overridden by a handful of people who want to sit in the playground drinking beer. If a community thinks it is wrong for teenagers to hang out in the streets in the evening, it should be able to pass anti-loitering laws that express its disapproval of this behavior – just it can ban smoking in public buildings to express its disapproval of this self-destructive behavior.

When modernist liberals say the anti-loitering laws restrict freedom, they are thinking of the personal freedom of the people who are loitering and ignoring the political freedom of people who cannot make decisions about how the public places in their own neighborhoods are used. Because people cannot use the law to deal with the problem themselves, they must have the problem solved for them by psychologists, youth workers, and other therapeutic experts.

Freedom of Speech to Freedom of Expression

During the 1960s, freedom of speech was also reinterpreted as a form of personal freedom. The classical view that free speech furthers the pursuit of truth was replaced with the modern view of speech as self-expression.

During most of the twentieth century, liberals were forced to defend serious political, scientific and literary speech from censorship: For example, McCarthyism was a threat to political speech through the 1950s, and an uncensored version of *Lady Chatterley's Lover* could not be published in the United States before 1959. However, as threats to serious speech began to fade,[176] liberals focused more and more strongly on obscenity.

The ACLU paved the way for this new approach in 1956, when it adopted the policy that the First Amendment protects all expression, that there is no special category of obscenity that is not protected.[177] Based on this policy, the ACLU fought for the idea that the First Amendment protects not only free speech but free expression – that is, not only words and ideas but also dancers at topless bars and films of sex acts. This may not have been exactly what the founders had in mind when they wrote the First Amendment to protect free speech.[178]

Like the other examples in this chapter, this new view of free speech was meant to expand freedom. Not only political speech is protected, but all speech, including obscenity. Not only speech is protected, but all forms of expression, including live sex shows. But, like the other examples in this chapter, the modernist view expands freedom by making it empty: It redefines speech as a form of private satisfaction rather than as public action.

Without quite understanding what he was saying, Charles Rembar, the lawyer who defended *Lady Chatterley's Lover*, *Tropic of Cancer*, and *Fanny Hill*, in a series of cases that he thought would overturn obscenity laws completely, gave this justification for free speech:

> ...thought is frustrated and tends to rot if it is contained in the individual. ... Aside from the collective benefit that comes from the free interchange of ideas, there is a direct personal benefit for the person concerned. Each of us should have the right to speak his thoughts.... It makes us feel good.[179]

Freedom of speech is important for the same reason as sexual freedom: Repression causes neurosis, and acting on our impulses makes us feel good. Madonna made the same point in a song about political activism, which included the lyrics:

Doctor King, Malcolm X
Freedom of Speech is as good as sex

and she knew better than Rembar that she was saying something that undermined the real function of speech.

During the 1960s, some places moved from the classical to the modernist view of free speech almost overnight. The Berkeley Free Speech Movement was organized to defend classical freedom of speech, the right of political groups to set up tables on campus to spread their ideas. But it was succeeded almost immediately by the Dirty Speech Movement: Students demonstrators carried signs that had nothing but obscenities written on them. These students thought they were trying to push freedom of speech as far as possible, but they actually were emptying freedom of speech of content.

Because of this change in the meaning of freedom of speech, American cities today cannot ban sex shops and businesses that let you "Talk to a Live Nude Girl," though they can use the zoning laws to control where they are located.[180] But this form of free expression has nothing at all to do with the classical view that free speech is the right to advocate any idea, however offensive, as part of a public debate that can lead to the truth. By defending this sort of thing as free speech, modernist liberals reinterpreted freedom as the right of isolated individuals to act in ways that give them private satisfactions – and they deprived people of the much more important right to govern themselves, to use the law to set standards of behavior in their own communities.

Of all the modernist reinterpretations of freedom, this one is the most interesting philosophically.

The classical defense of free speech, from Socrates to John Milton, is, first, that we have an obligation to speak the truth, and second, that freedom of speech is central to democracy, which depends on public discussion of what is a good life and a good society. Justice Brandeis still took this classical philosophical framework for granted in 1927, when he said, "freedom to think as you will and to speak as you think are means indispensable to the discovery of political truth.... Public discussion is a political duty...."[181]

By contrast, the modernist theory – which pragmatist and post-modernist philosophers state explicitly – is that ideas are nothing more than adjuncts to actions: Ideas are used to exercise power over nature or over other people. In this modernist view, speech has no transcendent truth value. It has a practical value, like any other action. Freedom of speech cannot be defended because it lets people find what Brandeis called "political truth": It has to be defended in the same way that freedom of action is defended.[182]

Debates over "hate speech" show that post-modernism has threatened the free discussion of ideas by eliminating the distinction between speech and action.

Feminists such as Catherine MacKinnon and Andrea Dworkin have claimed that pornography is not protected by the First Amendment, because it is not only speech but is also an action that harms women by degrading them, but American courts have not accepted this argument.[183] During the 1980s and 1990s, more than 350 American universities chilled the free discussion of ideas by adopting very broad rules against "hate speech" that degrades women and minority groups, based on the idea that this speech is a form of action, a sort of assault against minorities, but these bans have also not done well in American courts.[184]

The left split on free speech issues because modernists think of speech as self-expression and have forgotten the classic defense of free speech. On one side, civil libertarians want to carry self-expression – of both ideas and actions – as far as possible. On the other side, some feminists and multiculturalists want to ban ideas that hurt minorities or women, just as we ban actions that hurt minorities or women.

The classical defense of free speech, that open discussion of ideas lets the truth come out, provides a clear standard for when speech should be protected. A statement should be protected if it claims to be true.

For example, the statement "There is a global conspiracy of Jewish bankers" is protected, but the statement "You dirty Jew" is not. The statement "Homosexuality is immoral" is protected, but the statement "You faggot" is not. In both cases, the first statement is meant to be true: If we can ban the statement that there is a conspiracy of Jewish bankers because it offends people, then we can also ban serious studies of corporate power or political corruption when they offend people. But in both cases, the second statement has no truth value at all: It uses words purely as epithets, as expressions of hatred, not to make a statement that is true or false.

The grammatical form of the statement is not what is important. If you change these statements to "You are a dirty Jew" or "You are a faggot" they still should not be protected, because they are not meant as part of a discussion whose aim is to find the truth. Likewise, if a college professor makes statements that are sexual harassment of his students, this speech is pure action that should not be protected by the First Amendment, even if it is stated in sentences that are true or false, such as "You are beautiful," and "I want to make love to you." But if a professor argues seriously that women are inferior to men because they are different psychologically, he should be protected by the First Amendment, even if women in his class claim the statement is sexual harassment because it makes them feel uncomfortable.

The key difference is that, if a statement claims to be true, then it can be countered with more speech showing that it is false, but if speech does not claim to be true, it cannot be countered with more speech. If a professor tells his students that homosexuals or women are inferior, it is possible to produce evidence that shows his statement is false. But if a professor tells one of his students, "You are a faggot" or "I want to make love to you," you would miss the point if you tried to argue that his statements are false – that the first student is not really a homosexual and that the professor does not really want to make love with the second student. These statements are speech as action, not speech as part of a discussion that can lead to truth.

Modernist liberals cannot distinguish between these two sorts of speech: The ACLU wants to protect them both, and the censors of hate speech want to ban them both.

The civil libertarians thought they were expanding freedom of speech when they redefined it as freedom of expression, but now we can see that they have threatened our freedom by reducing speech to nothing more than expression.

The controversy over hate speech also shows that a liberal society cannot be based solely on the principle of negative freedom, the principle that people have a right to do whatever they please unless it harms someone else. Groups working against hate speech want to censor ideas that harm them – and they can make a plausible argument that the ideas do harm them. The principle of negative freedom does not offer a standard that we can use to protect free speech from these groups' attempts at censorship.

The standard we have suggested does not protect many forms of speech that were not traditionally protected by the First Amendment, including blackmail and fraud as well as obscenity. However, it does go further than the traditional idea that the First Amendment gives special protection to political speech, which is needed for self-government, by giving the same sort of special protection to all speech that is meant to be true. In addition to political speech, for example, this standard protects scientific theories: Galileo should have had the absolute right to say that the planets revolve around the sun, though this is not political speech. This classical liberal view of freedom of speech means that there should be no law that prevents the open discussion of ideas in pursuit of the truth, no matter how offensive and no matter how threatening to current institutions of society those ideas may be.

Modernism and Powerlessness

Modernist liberals believe they are expanding freedom by fighting against laws that are coercive, laws that directly limit personal action. This idea made sense in the past – direct coercion was the most important threat to freedom until the twentieth century – but modern technological societies have invented a new threat to freedom that is almost the opposite of coercion.

The model of domination in modern societies is television. No one coerces people to watch television. People become dependent on television because it is easier than making the effort to do something for yourself.

The modern economy as a whole makes people passive and dependent in the same way, and modernist liberals have deepened this dependence. Modernists believe that, in a technological society, the system should provide jobs, provide health care, provide education, provide child care, and provide social services for the public. Even without any coercion, people become dependent on these centrally managed services, because it is easier than managing your own business affairs, protecting your own health, raising your own children, or helping to govern your own neighborhood.

Because modernists think only of negative freedom, freedom from direct government coercion, they do not see that we lose the positive freedom to do things for ourselves when the technological system takes over all the responsibilities of individuals, families, and local communities,. Americans watch politicians on television rather than speaking out publicly themselves, they work at nine-to-five jobs rather than managing their own business affairs, and they depend on day-care centers and schools rather than raising their own children. But our civil libertarians say nothing about the ways that modernization has made us powerless: They seem to think that Americans would be freer than ever before, if only they had an unlimited right to loiter on street corners and buy pornography.

Liberals Move Beyond Modernism

Yet there was another side of the left of the sixties and seventies that was very much the opposite of modernist. There was widespread criticism of centralization and of consumerism.

The change in the left's way of thinking is most obvious if we look at its changing view of the Amish. The Bohemian socialists, at the beginning of the twentieth century, would have considered the Amish a symbol of everything they hated most: The repressive, traditional, Puritanical way of life that they hoped modernization would sweep away. Since the 1970s, though, the left has admired the Amish as a symbol of simpler living, of self-reliance, and of independence from the modern economic system.

In general, the side of 1960s radicalism that criticized modernization did not affect mainstream politics. There were many academic criticisms of the technological society during the 1960s and 1970s – such as Christopher Lasch's criticisms of the helping professions and John Holt's criticisms of public schooling – but also they did not have any practical effect on mainstream liberal politics.

There is only one case where this radical criticism of technology entered the liberal mainstream and made Americans more willing to do for themselves: health care. During the 1960s and 1970s, radical critics of high-tech medicine, such as Ivan Illich,[185] argued that we had reached a point where we were no longer improving health by spending more on doctors and hospitals. They said that, now, the most important way to improve our health is by eating a better diet, exercising, and giving up smoking.

As a result, the political rhetoric about health is very different from the rhetoric about other issues. Conservatives often criticize liberals for being morally lax – soft on crime and willing to tolerate teenage sex, drug use, and other irresponsible behavior – but when it comes to health, conservatives accuse the left of being too Puritanical. They complain about anti-smoking laws and about the "food police," and they try to annoy liberals by talking about how much they enjoy smoking a good cigar after eating a steak dinner.

Yet the case where liberals are Puritanical is the case where things got better. Life expectancy increased sharply during the 1970s and 1980s, largely because Americans smoked less, ate less saturated fat, and exercised more.

Because people still feel they have some control over their own bodies, even though they feel powerless to act in the public realm, health is the one area where liberals have gone beyond modernism. The Bohemian socialists and the flaming youth of the 1920s placed drinking and smoking high on the list of the new freedoms that they claimed – particularly for women. – and during the 1960s, drug use was added to the list. This is the modernist idea of personal freedom – that you have a right to do anything to your own body as long you do not hurt someone else – and it goes along with the modernist idea that health care is a technical problem that the medical system should deal with. When the critics of high-tech medicine said that people should take care of their own health, they rejected the modernists' negative idea of freedom and moved back toward a positive idea of freedom: Freedom is the ability to do something significant yourself, to improve your own health.

This new positive idea of freedom made liberals support anti-smoking laws, using the law in a way that modernist liberals reject. Like laissez-faire liberals, modernist liberals believe that the law should protect everyone's rights and guarantee everyone fair treatment, but that it should remain morally neutral and not pass judgment on people's personal behavior. By contrast, anti-smoking laws enforce common values: At first, these laws were framed in the language of moral neutrality – restaurants were required to have smoking and non-smoking sections, so that people could choose which they wanted – but soon they went further, and smoking was completely banned in public buildings, stores, and offices. These laws are used to make the statement that society is against smoking – to stigmatize smokers by requiring them to leave the building if they want a cigarette – and they helped to cause a decline in smoking and improvement in health.

Laws against smoking in public places are meant to change smokers' behavior by using the law to make it clear that the community disapproves of smoking. These laws do not invade people's privacy by trying to prevent them from smoking in their own homes, but they do move beyond the key idea of laissez-faire and modernist liberalism, that the "procedural republic" should protect citizens' rights to pursue their own interests and should remain neutral about the personal choices that citizens make. Anti-smoking laws do not protect each individual's right to pursue private satisfactions; they assert our common values.

Modernist liberals usually hate this sort of "coercive" law, and it is interesting that we do not hear the same complaints about anti-smoking laws that we hear about anti-loitering laws, anti-pornography laws, and other laws that regulate people's personal behavior in public places. Liberals do not say that anti-smoking laws are a short term fix for deeper problems,[186] and we should change society to eliminate the causes of smoking. They do not say that we should feel compassion and tolerance for cigarette smokers, and spend money on programs to help them rather than stigmatizing and criminalizing them. Instead, they are willing to pass laws that force people to go outside to smoke – stigmatizing smokers because of their personal behavior.

This is the one case where we have moved beyond negative freedom. We see that freedom is not the absence of coercion; it is the ability to do significant things for yourself. Though laissez-faire and modernist liberals would call them coercive, laws that ban smoking in public places actually increase positive freedom, by encouraging people to take care of their own health. Because they are based on a positive idea of freedom rather than a negative idea of freedom, anti-smoking laws actually succeeded in improving health.

Chapter 6
After Modernism

During the early and mid-twentieth century, Americans had great faith in economic progress, and liberals led the movement to bring the blessings of modernization to everyone. From the New Deal through the Great Society, liberals believed big government should balance the power of big business in order to spread the benefits of the modern economy widely. As big business became more centralized and more efficient, government would also become more centralized and would take advantage of the wealth that businesses generate to fund social programs that provide everyone with jobs, housing, health care, education, and other services.

Today, no one has the technological optimism that buoyed liberals and leftists during most of the twentieth century.

In part, modernism failed because centralized bureaucracies turned out to be less efficient than expected. The Soviet Union collapsed because its centrally planned economy did not work. Countries all over the world privatized industries that they had socialized a few decades earlier, to make their economies more efficient. In America, centralized programs to help people did not always work: Many urban housing projects built during the 1960s have been torn down.

Modernism also failed because modernization became less attractive as we moved from a scarcity economy to a surplus economy.

In the year 1900, the average American had an income near what we now call the poverty line.[187] Many people lacked even basic health care. Public schools had classes with 50 students or more. Urban workers in the United States lived in over-crowded tenements, where the inner rooms had no windows and where all the apartments on a floor shared one toilet. At the same time, business was becoming more centralized and was using new mass-production technology to increase production rapidly. Liberals wanted government to use similar methods to provide everyone with the essentials of a decent life, such as basic health care, education, and housing. For example, public school systems expanded dramatically and provided children with education that was improved but was also standardized.

But in the year 2000, the average American's income was more than seven times what it was in 1900 (after correcting for inflation).[188] The mass-production model of society, where big government would provide everyone with standardized worker's housing, standardized public education and standardized government health care, is no longer appealing in our more affluent economy. This affluence gives people more choices; for example, Americans can plausibly choose to live in urban apartments, in row houses, in streetcar suburbs, or in auto-dependent suburbs.

International surveys of values, analyzed by Ronald Inglehart, show that there has been a generational change in attitudes, because older generations grew up facing scarcity and younger generations grew up in the affluent post-war economy. Older generations believe strongly in economic growth, but younger generations put more emphasis on quality of life. Older generations support centralized bureaucracies, but younger generations want to make more decisions for themselves, because they are better educated and more likely to work at jobs where they think for themselves.[189] Over the decades, these new attitudes have become dominant in many countries, as older generations have died off, but liberals continued to support centralized social programs – federal bureaucracies to provide universal preschool are one extreme example – not seeing that this modernist approach was popular a century ago but is much less popular today.

Today, economic growth brings fewer benefits than it did a century ago, because most Americans already have enough to be economically comfortable. After you have decent education, health care, and housing, there is much less benefit to spending more on these things than there was in the days when many Americans had little schooling, no health care, and slum housing. In fact, international surveys of self-reported happiness show that higher income increases happiness in poorer countries, but that there is no longer any connection between higher income and happiness after a nation's average income reaches about half the level of the average American income today.[190]

At the same time that it brings decreasing benefits, economic growth brings increasing problems – worldwide problems such as global warming and high energy prices, and local problems such as traffic congestion and suburban sprawl.

As economic growth brings diminished benefits and increased costs, liberalism must change by developing policies that let us make a transition to an age of slower growth. Rather than the modernist liberal policies that stimulate growth to provide people with more jobs, more housing, more health care, and more education, we need policies that give people the choice of downshifting economically and doing more for themselves. We need to recognize that, after we have reached the point where we are economically comfortable, the most important ways to improve our lives involve doing more for ourselves rather than consuming more.

In earlier chapters, we have seen how the need to accommodate economic growth undermined the classical liberal idea of positive freedom. Laissez-faire liberals reduced people's ability to make political decisions about the sort of society they lived in, because many of these decisions were left to the market. Modernist liberals reduced people's ability to make both political decisions and also to make many significant decisions about their own lives, because they believe these decisions must be made by experts who manage centralized bureaucracies that provide them with goods and services; people only had the freedom to make decisions about narrowly personal behavior.

This chapter will sketch some policies that increase people's positive freedom – policies that allow people to make more decisions for themselves and to do more for themselves. It will look at significant individual choices that people can make about their own standard of living, their own health care, and their children's education, and it will look at significant political choices that people can make about the sorts of cities they live in and about other aspects of the public realm.

Liberals have focused on negative freedom for so long that we overlook these sorts of choices, though they are essential to let us move beyond the rapid-growth economy that laissez-faire liberalism and modernist liberalism promoted, and instead shift toward a more sustainable economy.

The ideals of classical liberalism that were displaced to accommodate growth have become relevant again. Of course, we will not move back to a Jeffersonian economy where people manage their own small farms and small businesses. But people should be able to make significant economic and political decisions once again, after a long hiatus when these decisions were ignored to maximize economic growth.

Individual Choice

First we will look at some examples where we should allow more individual choice.

On many of these issues, today's liberals still take the same modernist approach that they took one hundred years ago. They want to help people by stimulating the economy and setting up centralized bureaucratic organizations to provide services.

If we look at a few examples, we will be able to see why setting up massive bureaucracies to provide services made sense a century ago, when there was a scarcity economy, but no longer makes sense in today's more affluent economy. Instead, today's liberals should be developing social policies that promote positive freedom. We look at these examples briefly here, but I have written about them at greater length in other books.[191]

Downshifting Economically

A century ago, it made some sense to demand that the federal government stimulate economic growth to provide more jobs. In a scarcity economy, the growth was needed and the jobs were useful.

In today's surplus economy, with looming environmental problems, we should be developing policies that give people the option of "downshifting" economically, working shorter hours and earning less in order to have more time for themselves.

The idea that the federal government should stimulate the economy to create more jobs is the basis of modern American economic policy. Liberals initiated it – it was the central idea of the New Deal – but it is now an issue where there is absolute agreement among all mainstream politicians, from liberal to conservative. Yet today's liberals face a real self-contradiction between this conventional policy, which they have supported for many decades, and the new policies that we need to deal with ecological limits to growth.

Compulsory Growth

Our economic policy during most of the last century has been based on the idea that economic growth is compulsory, because it is needed to create jobs and to avoid unemployment that would cause widespread suffering. The United States has generally aimed for an economic growth rate of 3% to 3.5%, and when growth was slower than this, unemployment has increased. Though we may not realize it, we believe that we must produce more, whether or not we want the products, purely in order to create extra work for ourselves.

During the 1930s, economists blamed the Depression on inadequate consumer demand, and the New Deal began funding freeways, suburban housing, and other public works, in order to stimulate the economy and create jobs. During the post-war period, in the wake of the Depression, everyone agreed that we needed to promote economic growth to create more jobs. Businesses stepped up their advertising. The federal government stimulated the economy through deficit spending, funding for freeway construction, and policies to encourage development of suburban housing.

Earlier in the twentieth century, some liberal economists had developed a different view of economic growth: They said that growth would slow when demand was satiated – when people had all the goods and services that they needed. For example, Keynes wrote in his famous essay, "Economic Possibilities for Our Grandchildren" that there had been no great change in the average person's standard of living throughout recorded history, until technological innovation and the accumulation of capital caused sustained economic growth in modern Europe and America. As a result of this growth, scarcity no longer was a permanent problem for the human race, as it had always been, so that "a point may soon be reached ... when these [economic] needs are satisfied in the sense that we prefer to devote our further energies to non-economic purposes." Then, he predicted, "man will be faced with his real, his permanent problem – how to occupy the leisure which science and compound interest have won for him ...."[192]

From the nineteenth century through the 1930s, labor unions supported a shorter work week. During the Depression, unions argued that shorter hours would let us avoid unemployment by sharing necessary work, rather than by creating unnecessary work; William Green, president of the AFL was the leading advocate of this view. Shorter hours would also give workers more time for their families, for cultural activities, and for do-it-yourself projects that would give them the satisfaction that work longer provided now that factory production had replaced crafts production.

To deal with unemployment caused by the Depression, labor supported the Black-Connery bill, which would have reduced the work-week to 30 hours. The Senate passed this bill in 1933. It was stopped in the House of Representatives by fierce opposition from business interests, who said that we should fight unemployment by spreading a "new gospel of consumption" rather than by shortening work hours.[193]

Liberals' support for shorter work hours was forgotten during the postwar period, when everyone believed in stimulating growth and providing jobs. It has begun to reappear during the last decade: European countries have started promoting shorter work hours to reduce unemployment and help people balance work with family, and economists such as Juliet Schor have made the obvious point that ecological constraints require shorter work hours and slower growth.[194]

Choice of Work Hours

In today's economy, most people have little or no choice of work hours. Most good jobs are full-time, and most part-time jobs have low wages and no benefits.

Among males, average hourly earnings of part-time workers are less than 40% of the hourly earnings of full-time workers, and only 15% of part time workers have medical benefits. Juliet Schor has calculated that, if a typical male worker shifted from a full-time to a half-time job, he would lose 80% of his income.[195] Surveys of men have shown that 85% do not have any choice of work hours: Their only choice is a full-time job or no job.[196]

We need policies that give people a choice of work hours, and there are many possible incentives that we could offer to encourage businesses to provide well paying part time jobs. The ideal policy is already in place in Netherlands and Germany, which give full-time employees the right to request part-time work and require employers to accommodate these requests unless they can show that it would cause economic hardship to the business. In addition, the entire European Union has a policy forbidding discrimination against part-time workers, so employers must give them equivalent pay to full-time workers.

Largely because of these policies, the average Dutch employee works only about 70% as many hours per year as the average American employee.[197] The Dutch work so much less than Americans, in part, because they live in row houses rather than sprawl suburbs, they bicycle rather than driving as their main form of transportation, and so on. In the Netherlands, each person has the choice of working shorter hours and earning less, and many people have deliberately made this choice of living more simply in order to have more time.

With choice of work hours, people can decide how much to work based on how much income they need, deliberately choosing their standard of living. All of these decisions individuals make about what standard of living they want, would add up to determine the total GDP, the standard of living of the country as a whole. People could decide to take some of their productivity and wage gains in the form of shorter work hours rather than in the form of more goods and services, so there could be a slow-growth economy without rising unemployment.

Economic planning would still be needed to fine tune the economy to avoid unemployment and inflation. As the Canadian economist Peter Victor has shown, we would need new macroeconomic policies to manage a slow-growth economy.[198] But the planners should manage the economy so it gives people the amount of work they want – rather than promoting growth purely to create extra work.

Cultural Change

The shift to shorter work hours and slower growth would require a major cultural change.

Part of this cultural change would be a move toward what Juliet Schor sometimes calls "post-materialist values."[199] Differences in values have a real effect on macroeconomic policy: According to international surveys, the Netherlands has the most post-materialists – post-materialists outnumber materialists by 26% of the population – and the Netherlands has also done the most to shorten work hours.[200]

Part of this cultural change would involve recognizing that, after we have become economically comfortable, many of the most important things we can do to enhance our well being are things that we do for ourselves. For example, as we will see, the most important thing we can do to improve our health is to exercise more and improve our diets, but the typical American today does not have enough time to exercise.

Part of this cultural change would be making better use of our leisure time – but here we have been moving in the wrong direction. In 1930, Kellogg's implemented a 30 hour work week at its factory in Battle Creek, Michigan, as an experiment in work sharing during the depression, and surveys showed that the workers generally spent the extra free time reading, visiting with family and friends, in community activities such as amateur sports, clubs, and churches, in adult education courses, in gardening and other do-it-yourself projects. Many considered the extra leisure "the most important part of the day."[201] But from the 1950s onward, surveys showed that Kellogg's workers were increasingly likely to use their extra leisure passively, for example, watching television or movies: Their attitude was that they have done their important work for the day, and it was time for them to relax and be entertained.[202]

To reduce work hours, we need to reject the modern idea that leisure is time for relaxation and passive amusement, and to return to the classical view of leisure. Aristotle put it most clearly by saying that leisure is more valuable than work because leisure activities are ends in themselves, while work is merely a means to an end. We work to live, but we use our leisure to live well. Classically, leisure was used for music, politics, conversation, study, sports, and the like; today, we can drop the classical bias against manual labor and also use leisure for productive activities that are satisfying in themselves, such as gardening, crafts, and caring for our own children.

Liberals have begun to talk about shorter work time during the last decade, and it is bound to become a central issue during the coming century. Many people will continue to devote their lives to getting and spending money, but if a significant number of people decide they want to downshift, to produce and consume less so they have more time to do for themselves, it would make a major contribution to our efforts to fight global warming and other ecological threats.

Protecting Our Own Health

A century ago, it made some sense to call for a federal bureaucracy to provide everyone with health care. Most people could not afford even the primitive medical care that was available at the time, and setting up a centralized health-care bureaucracy was the quickest way to give everyone basic health care. This was done in some

European countries, which set up national health services after World War II.

Before the recent health-care reforms, providing universal health care was the most important unfinished business of the modernist liberal agenda, but the reforms passed under the Obama administration will provide at least 95% of Americans with health care, by forbidding insurers to deny coverage based on current condition, by requiring most people to buy health insurance if they are not covered by their employers, by giving subsidies to low-income people who cannot afford health insurance, and by expanding Medicare to cover those who cannot afford insurance even with subsidies.

We still need to improve these policies to cover 100% of Americans, but liberals should also focus on dealing with the central problem of our health care system: Americans spend twice as much on health care as the average in industrialized nations, but we have lower life expectancy and higher infant mortality than the average in industrialized nations. We need to develop policies that bring us up to the level of other industrialized nations, both by reducing wasteful spending and improving our health.

Spending More on Health Care

The underlying cause of America's high medical costs is the cost-plus health insurance system put in place during the post-war period, when Americans were flush with affluence and had boundless faith in technology. Under this system, it was up to the doctor to decide that a treatment is needed, and the cost was passed through to the insurance company. Under this system, both the doctor and the health-care consumer ignore costs.[203]

A few wasteful medical treatments became notorious during the post-war period. Doctors removed children's tonsils at the first sign of trouble, for example, and studies showed that 90% of all tonsillectomies were not necessary.[204] Even worse, doctors routinely used X-rays as part of their regular checkups of young children: These have little value as a diagnostic tool, but they do cause cancer.

Tonsillectomies and X-rays became notorious and have been controlled, but researchers trying to control medical costs have identified many other wasteful treatments. During the 1980s, the Rand Corporation released the results of a series of studies that began by developing a consensus among doctors about when certain procedures were necessary, and then looked at thousands of case records to see how many procedures were performed unnecessarily. They found, for example, that of the 1,300 operations to remove athero-sclerotic plaque from the carotid artery of elderly patients that were studied, 32% were inappropriate; Of the 386 coronary bypass operations studied, 14% were inappropriate.

Some members of the Rand research team founded Value Health Sciences, which did extensive studies of high-volume procedures. These studies showed, for example, that about half of all Cesarean sections performed in the United States are inappropriate. This is the most common surgical procedure in the United States. Likewise, they found that 27% of all hysterectomies are inappropriate. This is the second most common major surgical procedure in the United States, and gynecologists regularly recommend hysterectomies for fibroids, uterine prolapse, and heavy bleeding, though there are less dangerous treatments for all of these.

The studies by Rand corporation and Value Health Sciences ignored cost and said a procedure was inappropriate only if its risk to the patient was greater than its benefit – that is, only it if actually harmed the health of the average patient. Studies like these, which look at individual procedures to see which are unnecessary, estimate that one-quarter to one-third of our health care spending is wasted.[205]

International comparisons show that even more is wasted. The United States spends more than twice as much per capita on health care as the average for the Organization for Economic Cooperation and Development (made up of the world's industrialized nations); but, among the 24 countries in the OECD, the United States ranks 21st in infant mortality, 17th in male life expectancy, and 16th in female life expectancy. Comparing ourselves with other industrial nations, we have to conclude that we could be healthier than we are even if we spent just half as much.

Reforming Health Insurance

America's health care costs have exploded during the past few decades – from 5.3% of the GDP in 1960 to over 17% of the GDP today – though per capita GDP is far higher today than it was in 1960. Insurance companies and Health Maintenance Organizations have tried to control costs for decades by restricting which providers and procedures they cover. By imposing Draconian cost controls, which cause tremendous frustration to both doctors and patients, they have slowed but not stopped the growth in medical spending.

Liberals continue to talk about top-down policies to control cost, but some conservatives have proposed health-insurance reforms that could control costs by letting people make decisions about their own health care. Conservatives have developed proposals to replace comprehensive health insurance with a combination of catastrophic health insurance for major expenses and Medical Savings Accounts to pay smaller expenses.

John Goodman and Gerald Musgrave, who developed the most important of these conservative plans,[206] pointed out that, during the 1990s, when they wrote, comprehensive health coverage for a family typically cost about $4,500 per year, while health coverage with a $2,000 deductible typically cost $1,800. Rather than providing comprehensive coverage, employers could save money by paying $1,800 for insurance and also giving employees $2,000 to put in Medical Savings Accounts, which they could use to pay the deductible expenses. People would keep any extra money left in their Medical Savings Accounts, giving them an incentive not to spend this money wastefully. They could withdraw some excess funds from these accounts after they retired, and they could leave the balance to their heirs after they died.

Insurance with a high deductible costs less overall, because people are less likely to use health care wastefully when they are spending their own money.

Conservative plans do have too much faith in the free market. Goodman and Musgrave, and many other conservatives, have suggested giving people allowances that let them purchase their own health insurance. Liberals have been right to reject this idea because risk pools are needed to make insurance available to everyone. If everyone got a fixed sum to pay for their own insurance, insurance companies would offer coverage at a reasonable cost only to people who are healthy, and people who are unhealthy would not be able to afford insurance.

But the need for risk pools does not justify liberals' blanket opposition to Medical Savings Accounts: We could change employee or government health-insurance programs so that they offer everyone fully funded Medical

Savings Accounts. If a company provided this sort of plan to all of its employees, paying for insurance with a high deductible and giving employees an allowance to put in their Medical Savings account that is large enough to pay the entire deductible, all employees would be covered at a significantly lower cost.

This reform is one example of the direction we should be moving. We should go beyond the modernist approach of creating centralized bureaucracies that make decisions for us, and instead we should let people make decisions for themselves, giving them the option of spending less on their own health care and keeping the savings.

Living Healthier Lives

This insurance plan would lower costs, but to improve health, we also need to convince people to change their habits and live healthier lives. For example, 68% of American adults are overweight and 34% are obese, double the percentage of 30 years ago.[207] It is now generally recognized that obesity has become one of our greatest health problems, an important cause of heart disease, strokes, and diabetes.

We need a public education campaign to tell the public about the danger of obesity and the benefits of exercise and low fat diets, similar to the public education campaign about the dangers of cigarette smoking. As one part of this campaign, we could require warning labels on high-fat foods, similar to the warnings on cigarettes. For example, if packaged food or fast food gets more than 30% of its calories from fat, it could be required to have a label saying "Warning: High Fat," and if it gets more than 50% of its calories from fat, it could be required to have a warning label saying "Warning: Very High Fat. Can contribute to obesity, which is a cause of heart disease and diabetes."

We also need to tax unhealthy foods to discourage people from eating them. There have been several proposals to tax sugary beverages: For example, New York State proposed a tax of one cent per ounce, which was expected to cut consumption of sugary beverages by 15%, but this law was defeated because of a heavy advertising campaign by the group named New Yorkers Against Unfair Taxes, which was funded by soda manufacturers and bottlers. In reality, this would be an eminently fair tax: New York spends about $7.5 billion per year treating medical conditions related to obesity, and this tax would have raised about $1 billion per year, making people whose habits cause obesity pay a bit more of the cost of treating obesity.[208]

Changing people's habits is the most important thing we can do to improve health. It is far less expensive and more effective than providing medical technology to patch people up after they get sick. It promotes positive freedom, the sense that we can act to improve our own health.

Many Americans also need more free time to be able to improve their own health. Many people do not have time to exercise and depend on fast food because they do not have time to cook for themselves or their families. A change in our attitude toward our health could also change our attitude toward our work and consumption generally: When it comes toward our health, it should be clear that we would be better off if we rejected consumerism, worked shorter hours, and had more time to exercise and eat well – improving our health by doing for ourselves.

Raising Our Own Children

A century ago, it made some sense to demand that the government spend more money to provide everyone with better schooling. Classes in urban public schools were overcrowded, and only 6% of Americans were high-school graduates. More funding was badly needed to give the average person a decent education.

Today, liberals still make the old demands for more spending on education, and they have added the demand for more spending to provide universal preschool. Yet studies show that the amount of money spent on schooling is less important to academic achievement than the quality of family and community life. Liberals would do better to develop policies to deal with the fact that most parents feel they do not have enough time to spend with their preschool children.

Spending More on Education

Increased spending on education brought real benefits through the first half of the twentieth century. In 1900, classrooms in urban elementary schools often had 50 pupils. By 1960, average class size in elementary schools had declined to 31-32 pupils. At the same time, a massive expansion of high schools and colleges had opened educational opportunities that most people could hardly imagine before the twentieth century.

But during the 1960s and 1970s, academic achievement declined, even as spending continued to increase more quickly than ever.

Spending on education soared during the 1960s and 1970s. Between 1960 and 1975 alone, spending per student more than doubled (in real terms, after correcting for inflation);[209] spending today is more than four times what it was in 1960. Average class size in elementary schools went down from 31-32 in the 1960 to 26 per class today. Yet scores on standardized tests declined during the 1960s and 1970s, despite dramatically increased spending.[210]

By the 1960s and 1970s, we had reached a point where we spent enough on schooling: Spending more no longer brought significant benefits, so that higher educational achievement depended primarily on the family and community. The two definitive studies of the time, the famous Coleman report of the 1960s and Christopher Jencks study of inequality during the 1970s, both concluded that quality of schooling had a small effect on educational achievement, and that the most important factor affecting educational achievement (apart from innate aptitude) was the quality of family and community life.[211]

Likewise, a comprehensive review of the literature by Eric Hanushek of the University of Rochester found that students do not have higher achievement if their schools spend more money per pupil or have smaller class sizes, but that different teaching methods can affect achievement.[212] Lawrence Steinberg sums up the research by saying:

> When very gross measures of school quality are used – the amount of money in the school's budget, for example, or the number of books in the school's library – research tends to show that differences in school quality are not important .... When finer measures of school quality are used, however – measures that look closely at quality of classroom instruction, studies show that school practices can make a difference, albeit a modest one.[213]

In general, Steinberg says, students perform better in schools where teachers are supportive but firm and have high academic standards. But he adds that differences in quality of schooling are much less important than the family and the peer group.

International comparisons also show that spending more money on schooling no longer brings significant improvements in achievement. Studies by the Organization for Economic Cooperation and Development found that the United States spends almost 50% more per student than the average OECD country, but our student achievement is lower than the OECD average.[214]

During the 1960s and 1970s, we had reached a point where spending more on schooling was no longer the key to improving education, just as spending more on medical care was no longer the key to improving health: As in health care, improvement in education primarily on personal effort by the family, community, peer group, and student, rather than on increased spending.

Educational achievement declined during the 1960s and 1970s, in part, because many Americans became less able to raise their own children. Divorce and unwed motherhood increased, and even intact families had less time for their children, because most needed two incomes to support their standard of living.

In just a few decades, America changed from a society where "broken homes" were an aberration to a society where most children spend at least part of their childhood with a single parent. The number of births to unwed mothers rose from 6% in 1960 to about 40% today. The divorce rate tripled between 1960 and 1980, when it leveled off with almost half of all marriages ending in divorce.

During the 1960s and 1970s, modernist liberals believed that single motherhood was a valid alternative lifestyle, and that children recovered quickly from the emotional stress of divorce. Since then, social scientists have developed a body of solid research showing that unwed motherhood and divorce hurt children. The most extensive statistical analysis was done by Sara McLanahan and Gary Sandefur, who found that children of unwed or divorced parents are twice as likely to drop out of high school as children from intact families,[215] are 1.5 times as likely to be idle (out of school and out of work) as children from intact families,[216] and are almost twice as likely to become unwed mothers themselves as children from intact families.[217] Other studies have found that these children are also more liable to depression and eating disorders, are more likely to abuse alcohol and drugs, are more likely to become juvenile delinquents and adult criminals, and are more likely to be sexually abused than children from intact homes.[218]

The books *Open Marriage* and *Creative Divorce* were best sellers during the 1960s and 1970s, but today we can see today that children were the victims of their parents' search for "personal freedom."

Even in intact families, parents have less time for their children, because they are working harder and harder to maintain their standard of living. During the 1990s, parents spent 40% less time with their children than in 1965, primarily because they had to spend the extra time at work.[219] Most families feel they cannot afford to take care of their own preschool children, though surveys show that the overwhelming majority would prefer to, if it were economically possible.[220]

This is the failure of the modern economy that Americans feel most deeply. One hundred years ago, America's real per capita GDP was about one-seventh of what it is now, but virtually all families were able to care for their own children.[221] Yet now that we are so much wealthier, the majority of Americans feel that they cannot afford to care for their own preschool children.

Yet most liberals working on family policy demand more money for day care, more money for Head Start, more money for preschools, and more money for schooling – in other words, more money for programs provided by centralized bureaucracies, the modernist approach that made sense a century ago but is out of touch with today's reality. They do not ask why our standard of living demands so much work that parents have less time for their children, and they do not call for programs that would help parents care for their own children.

Reforming Child Care

Instead of demanding more money for bureaucratic programs that take over child raising, liberals should be looking for policies that give parents more time to be with their children.

There is no need to cut current levels of spending for education, as there is for health care, even though we spend more on education than other industrial nations and get worse results. We spend much less on education than on health care, about 6% of GDP compared with about 17%, and spending on education is not increasing so rapidly that it threatens our fiscal stability, as spending on health care is. We can afford the luxury of smaller classes for our children, even if they are not necessary to improve achievement.

But liberals do need to shift away from the single-minded focus on increased spending that dominates their current thinking about education. When it comes to child care, today's liberals carry the modernist approach even further than the liberals of a century ago. When Al Gore ran for president in 2000, he supported universal preschool for 3 and 4 year olds, a massive bureaucracy to provide more years of education that studies have shown does not benefit most children. And Hillary Clinton goes much further by supporting preschool for all children beginning at the age of four months.[222]

To shift away from this modernist approach, the most obvious thing we can do to provide non-discriminatory funding for child care, funding that goes equally to parents who use day care and to parents who care for their own preschoolers.

Virtually all of the funding we now provide for child care discriminates against parents who care for their own children: We subsidize day-care and preschools, but we give nothing to parents who take care of their own children. For example, there is a federal child-care tax credit available to parents who pay for day-care, but no tax credit for parents who work shorter hours to care for their own children. Federal tax laws encourage businesses to offer free or subsidized day-care to their employees, but not to give an equal subsidy to parents who care for their own children.

A dual-income couple gets a child-care tax credit and may get subsidized day-care from an employer. A couple trying to get by on a single income or on two part-time incomes does not get any subsidy at all, though they are making a much greater economic sacrifice to have the time to care for their children.

We should end this sort of discrimination by funding child care through a tax credit that goes to all parents of preschool children, not just to parents who use day care. Liberals typically call on the federal government to provide high-quality day care that costs about $10,000 per child per year. If we gave that money directly to families with preschool children as a tax credit, it would be enough to let most parents cut back on work and care for their own children, at least part time. People who need day care, such as single parents, could use this credit to pay for it, but the credit would give equal support to people who want to care for their own children.[223]

Some conservatives have backed this sort of approach to child care: For example, the first president Bush supported this approach during his presidential campaign of 1988, though he did nothing about it after being elected. Liberals would be very likely to get more funding for child care if they moved from their current demands for universal preschool to this approach of giving equal support to all parents of preschool children, because conservatives would find it hard to oppose funding that helps families care for their own children. We will not get a non-discriminatory tax credit as large as $10,000, any more than we will get the federal government to spend this much money on universal preschool, but we could get significant funding to support child care.

More Time for Our Children

In addition to funding that helps people spend more time with their children, we need a public education campaign to convince parents to make a more active effort to raise their own children. Preschool advocates claim that recent studies of the brain have shown us how to increase children's intelligence, but these studies actually just show that children's brains develop more rapidly if their parents hold them, play with them, sing to them, and – most important – talk to them. This is all that they do in preschool programs that have been shown to help poor, at-risk children, such as the Abecedarian Project.

Most middle-class parents already do these things with their children, which is why preschool does not improve achievement of middle-class children, but working class and poor parents are less likely to do these things. We could improve academic achievement of working class and poor children dramatically if we mounted a large public education campaign, including billboards and television ads, showing people how important it is to talk to your children, even when they are so young that they cannot understand what you are saying.[224]

In fact, if you look at the literature of groups that support more funding for preschools, you will find that they discuss brain science briefly to give their ideas a scientific veneer, and then they give examples of day care programs that do exactly what most middle-class parents already do – talk to infants before they have learned to speak, read to them, sing to them, give them interesting toys to play with, have affectionate interactions with them. You do not need a degree in brain science to do these things, but some parents need to be told how important it is to do these things.

Most Americans want more time to be with their children. A change in our attitude toward child care could help change our attitude toward our work and consumption generally: With our children, as with our health, we should recognize that we would be better off if we moderated our consumerism, worked shorter hours, and had more time to do for ourselves.

Supporting Voluntary Groups

We have looked at a few of many possible policies that could give people more positive freedom to make decisions about their own lives and their families. Just as centralized bureaucracies have undermined individuals' freedom to manage their own lives, they have also undermined civil society by taking over the functions of face-to-face groups.

We also need policies to revive voluntary organizations and to help them do some of the work that has been taken over by remote bureaucracies.

The most obvious way to restore public life is by providing matching government funds for voluntary groups that deal with social problems and for other charitable groups. George W. Bush took a step in this direction when he ran for president in 2000 and campaigned for "compassionate conservatism," with the federal government matching private donations to voluntary groups.

Unfortunately, liberals focused on Bush's plans to support faith-based organizations, which they opposed because of their modernist misinterpretation of the First Amendment, so the issue turned into a debate about separation of church and state. Liberals refused to see the obvious advantages of this sort of plan. It strengthens local communities. It allows a large number of different approaches to social problems to be tried on a small scale, so we can imitate the approaches that succeed and can discard the approaches that fail before they cause widespread damage. Not the least important, it may be the only politically feasible way of increasing funding for social programs, because it is supported by conservatives as well as liberals.

Liberals would do well to come up with their own proposals for funding voluntary groups. Conservatives support federal funding to match private donations of money to charities. Liberals should also support federal funding to match donations of volunteer time to charities. With this policy, groups that attract large numbers of volunteers would get matching federal funding to keep them going, like groups that attract money donations. This liberal approach is more democratic, because everyone who is willing to donate time has an equal ability to generate matching funds, while the conservative approach is more plutocratic, because the rich can give large donations, and the poor can afford to give little or nothing. This liberal approach would allow poor communities to organize groups to help themselves, volunteering their time to run the groups and getting federal matching funds to help pay the groups' expenses.

To avoid waste, the government should track the results of the programs it supports and develop standards that allow them to continue matching funding for effective groups but deny funding for ineffective groups.

In addition to helping the poor, the same model of matching funds for voluntary organizations could be used more generally to promote civil society. For example, the National Endowment for the Arts now decides at the federal level which arts organizations will get grants. Because experts in the arts make the decisions, funding goes to safe projects, such as major classical orchestras, and to projects in the avant garde style of the mid-twentieth century, which is now the accepted academic style. The arts would be much more diverse, and they would include some genuinely new ideas, if the federal government matched the money and time given to arts organizations by private donors, rather than having a national board decide which projects the government will support. Centralized decision making is particularly deadening to the arts, but the same approach could also be used for many types of voluntary groups.

These proposals to promote local voluntary groups depend, in part, on shorter work hours and economic downshifting. Like child care, local volunteer groups used to depend on the unpaid labor of women, so they thrived in the days before women were absorbed into the market economy. Families and civil society could flourish again if both men and women spent less time earning money in the market economy and instead had more free time to care for their own children and to volunteer in their communities.

Political Choice

We have looked at a number of policies that let people make individual decisions about their own work hours, their own health care, their own families' child care, and their own communities' civic organizations. Currently, we ignore these individual choices, because we depend on centralized organizations that provide jobs, provide health care, provide child care, and provide welfare for the poor. We believe we are helping people by providing them with these services, but we are inadvertently giving people less ability to control their own lives. We clearly should give people positive freedom to make decisions about their own lives when it is possible, such as these decisions about their own work hours, their own health care, and their own child care.

In addition to these individual decisions, we need policies that let people make political decisions about the public realm.

Laissez-faire liberals of the nineteenth century ignored these political decisions and wanted the free market to shape the public realm. Today, some conservative economists take a similar approach, updating it to deal with current concerns about the environment: To avoid making political decisions about the public realm, they want to put a price on the environmental costs of different technologies and tax them to reflects these costs. Then the prices people pay for these products would take into account their environmental costs as well as the costs of producing them. The market would take into account all the costs and benefits of different products, and in this view, the market would deal with environmental costs in the most efficient way possible, while direct government regulation is less efficient.

There are many cases where this approach is useful – and, in fact, is urgently needed. Most obviously, we need to put a price on greenhouse gas emissions, so the market can let us shift to clean energy as efficiently as possible. In this case, it clearly is possible to set a price on pollution: For example, if we need to reduce greenhouse gas emissions 80% by 2050 to avoid the worst effects of global warming, we can set a cap on emissions that gradually diminishes until 2050, and we can auction the emission permits for each year to set their price.

But there are other cases where it is not possible to subdivide and sell the right to pollute the public realm. In these cases we need to make political decisions about the public realm.

To give a small example, it does not make sense to say that we want only a little bit of cigarette smoke in restaurants, so we will issue a limited number of permits to smoke in restaurants and auction them off. Most people want to be able to go to restaurants with no smoke at all, because even a bit of smoke can reduce their enjoyment of their meal, so it makes sense for the majority to pass laws banning smoking in restaurants completely.

This small example is useful because (as we have seen) smoking is the one case where we have generally accepted laws that limit people's personal behavior in public places. And everyone can recognize the principle involved: There are some cases where it makes no sense to subdivide the public realm and sell off the right to pollute it, so it is necessary to make a political choice about the public realm. Either restaurants will be smoky or they will be smoke-free.

Now, we will look at much larger examples where it is necessary to make political choices about the public realm.

Cities and Political Choices

Automobiles dominate the public realm of most American cities. In my book *Unplanning: Livable Cities and Political Choices*, I highlight the political choices underlying urban design by using a thought experiment that looks at how cities would be designed if they were built with three different political limits on the automobile. Apart from the political decision about limiting the automobile, the thought experiment assumes that people can make individual choices about what sort of neighborhood they want to live in, and it assumes that residents prefer low densities, as many Americans do.

A Car-Free City

As the first ideal type, consider a ban on automobiles for personal transportation in the city, which could give us neighborhoods like the streetcar suburbs that were popular in America a century ago. Because Americans are wealthier now, virtually everyone who wanted to could live in neighborhoods like the streetcar suburbs where the minority of Americans who were middle-class lived before World War I.

These streetcar suburbs were a high point of American urban design. They had free-standing houses with small front yards and adequate backyards. Shopping streets and trolley lines were within easy walking distance of homes, and there were apartments above the stores on the main shopping streets. Stores offered delivery of groceries and other heavy goods, because people did not own private vehicles.

Compare this model with the suburbs we have in America today. Neighborhoods like the streetcar suburbs would be quieter and safer for children than today's auto-dependent suburbs, because they would have no cars. They would be more neighborly because people would walk to local shopping and parks and meet their neighbors along the way. They would be healthier because people would get regular exercise from walking and bicycling.

Transportation would be about equally convenient, because shopping, services, and public transit would be within easy walking distance of homes, and because distances would be much shorter in this higher density, more compact city. Residents would save large amounts of money because of lower transportation costs.

A City that Tames the Automobile

As a second ideal type, to illustrate the effect of a different limit on automobile use, consider a city with a speed limit of 12 mph to 15 mph for private vehicles, about the same speed as a bicycle. This limit would let people use cars for local trips – for example, for hauling groceries home – but people would use higher speed public transit for most longer trips within the city. The city would have extensive rail service to accommodate the demand for longer trips.

Bicycles and small electric vehicles similar to golf carts could travel along with the automobiles in the main traffic lanes, because traffic would be slow. Shopping streets would be quieter and safer for pedestrians than they are in today's cities. On residential streets, the city could make traffic even slower, so they would be safe places for children to play, like the *woonerfs* in the Netherlands.

Because private vehicles are slow, public transportation would be used for almost all commuting and regional shopping. Businesses would naturally tend to cluster around transit nodes, because most employees and customers would come by transit. In this case, also, transportation would be about as convenient as in today's cities, because there would be shopping near homes, and because distances would be shorter in this more compact city. Again, people would save money because of shorter transportation distances – though they obviously would not save as much as in the car-free city.

Suburbia that Works

As a third ideal type, consider a city with an even looser limit on automobile use, a speed limit of 25 or 30 miles per hour. If the city had a relatively high-speed commuter rail system, people could all live in houses with two-car garages on quarter-acre lots, as they do in today's sprawl suburbs.

But the region as a whole would be very different from today's suburbia. With no freeways or high-speed arterials, most commuting would shift to rail, so development would tend to cluster around the rail stations. Instead of freeway-oriented regional shopping malls, the city would have mixed-use shopping and office complexes (with plenty of parking) at rail stations – though there would also be some districts zoned to accommodate automobile-oriented big-box shopping.

This model is not at all radical: It is how our cities would have developed after World War II if we had decided to promote suburbanization by building rapid commuter rail systems rather than freeways. This third ideal type represents a deliberate, responsible political choice of today's suburban way of life: It would let everyone live in suburbia without blighting the entire region with freeways and traffic, and without blighting the earth with global warming.

Urban Design and Way of Life

The point of the thought experiment should be clear even from this brief summary: These different political choices create cities with different ways of life.

A 30 mile per hour speed limit would promote a way of life that focuses on the private satisfactions that you get from consuming. People would have houses on large lots and would have several cars for each family.

A ban on automobiles would promote a way of life that focuses on public goods rather than on private satisfactions. People would live on smaller lots and without automobiles in order to have a city that is quieter, safer, and more neighborly.

Within the framework of this political decision, people can also make individual decisions about how they want to live. These three models assume that people prefer low densities, as many Americans do. The results would be very different if people preferred dense urban neighborhoods, as many Europeans do.

People should make these decisions for themselves, because they are decisions about what sort of lives people want to live. The decision about limiting automobile use should be a political choice, because it is a decision about the public realm. The decision about what sort of housing to live in should be an individual choice.

These three limits are not meant as practical policies. Environmentalists have advanced many practical policies that would let us build more livable, less auto-dependent cities. These three limits are meant as a thought experiment to show that key decisions about urban design are not technical decisions that should be made by planners. They are human decisions about the sort of lives that we want to lead, and so they are decisions that we should all make.

Political Limits on Technology

There are some cases where we have already begun to make political decisions about the public realm. For example, environmentalists have had some success in limiting the use of off-road vehicles in the national parks. This is a case where we can all see that we need to make political decisions about the public realm: Just as restaurants are either smoky or smoke-free, the parks are either noisy or quiet. We can see that this is a political decision because it is a decision about what sort of life we want to live: Do we want to use the parks for contemplative walks that let us enjoy the quiet of nature, or do we want to go to the parks to get thrills by driving all-terrain vehicles or snowmobiles at high speeds? In any given place, we can only do one of these: If snowmobiles are allowed, the noise disturbs people who enjoy quiet.

There are other cases where this sort of political decision is just as obviously necessary, but environmentalists have not had success in protecting the public realm. For example, our lakes are filled with jet skis and motorboats, which annoy people who want to enjoy the quiet. Small private airplanes can fly virtually anywhere: If you move to a suburb to escape the city's noise, or if you go to a park to escape the city's noise for the day, you still cannot escape the noise of the small planes flying overhead.

The negative idea of freedom is one great obstacle to controlling technology.

We can see it at its worst in a television advertisement paid for by the Georgia Highway Contractor's Association. A Korean War veteran reads the lines:

> Environmentalists are telling us how to live our lives...preventing us from driving cars, and forcing us to live downtown. In America, these are still personal choices. Tyranny didn't win in South Korea. Don't let it get a foothold here.[225]

The advertisement defines freedom purely as a matter of making individual choices, and it ignores political choices. It does not mention that North Korea is a dictatorship and that America is a democracy – and that in a democracy, the voters should be able to make decisions about the public realm: For example, voters should be able to decide whether they want freeways or public transportation built in their city, rather than automatically accommodating individuals who choose to drive.

The ad says "in America, there are still personal choices," but it does not realize that a free society should also allow people to make political choices.

Conservatives use the laissez-faire ideal of freedom to argue against controlling technology. And the modernist idea of personal freedom is also operative, when it comes to technologies such as automobiles and off-road vehicles. In the early twentieth century, modernists loved speed and motion because it gave them a sense of personal freedom – you can see it most clearly in the drawings of the Italian futurists – and American still connect the automobile and off-road vehicle with the idea of "personal freedom."

We need to move beyond this negative idea of freedom, that the government should not stop people from doing whatever they feel like, to a positive idea of freedom, that people should be able to make significant individual decisions about their own lives and significant political decisions about the public realm.

Reducing Inequality

To reclaim the ideals of classical liberalism, we also need to reduce inequality. We have seen that increasing inequality repeatedly led to the decline and fall of republican governments since ancient times, so it is unsettling that inequality in the United States has increased so dramatically during the last few decades that it is now worse than in any other developed nation.

In 1981, the United States ranked thirteenth among 22 developed nations in income inequality. Today we rank last, the most unequal country in the developed world.[226] The top 10% of Americans make 48.5% of all income, almost as much as the remaining 90% of Americans. And the top one-tenth of 1% of Americans make as much income as the bottom 50% of Americans; that is, just 300,000 Americans at the top now make as much income half of all Americans combined.[227]

Inequality is caused partly by larger economic trends – globalization has eliminated most of the well-paying factory jobs that unskilled American workers could get decades ago – but changes in our tax system have made inequality much worse than it needs to be and much worse than it is in other industrial nations.

During the depression, the Roosevelt administration created a very progressive income tax system, with a maximum tax rate of 91% on income above $2 or $3 million a year in today's dollars. During the 1960s, liberals support for progressive taxation weakened, because it was a time of rapid economic growth, when it was tempting to avoid the political conflicts caused by redistributing income and instead rely on growth to help raise everyone's income. The Kennedy administration lowered the maximum tax rate to 70%, claiming that it was also eliminating loopholes for the rich that had been added to the tax system during the 1950s. During the 1980s, conservatives went much further: Claiming that lowering taxes would stimulate economic growth, the Reagan administration cut the maximum income tax rate to 27%. Adding to the unfairness of the tax system, Social Security taxes apply only to wages and salaries below a cut-off level, not to the highest salaries and not to earnings from investments, and many moderate income people pay more Social Security taxes than income taxes.

We could reduce inequality dramatically by returning to a more progressive income tax system, similar to the system we had before the Reagan era – not by increasing taxes but by changing tax rates so the very rich pay their fair share and the middle class pays less. In addition, we should expand the Earned Income Tax Credit for low and moderate income working people, so everyone who works earns a living wage.

Increased income inequality has also brought increased political inequality. Money has begun to dominate our politics in the same way it did in the late days of the Athenian, Roman and Florentine republic. We need political reforms to limit the ways that big money dominates politics.

The recent Supreme Court decision in Citizens United v. Federal Election Commission (2010) was a huge step in the wrong direction, ruling that the law cannot limit corporate funding of independent political advertising for candidates in elections. A conservative court based this decision on the idea of negative freedom: Freedom of speech means that government cannot limit anyone's speech – not only that the government cannot censor content but also that it cannot limit spending.

Liberals should counter this decision by developing an interpretation of the First Amendment based on positive freedom. The goal of the founders was to allow the free discussion of all ideas, because free discussion of ideas is necessary to democratic self-government. A long series of decisions found that the government can control the manner of speech though it cannot control the content of speech: For example, the law cannot prevent someone from advocating a specific idea, but it can prevent someone from advocating that idea by driving around the streets in a sound-truck at 4 AM with the amplifier turned to top volume. The courts should carry similar reasoning a step further by finding that we can control the amount of money spent on political advocacy though it cannot control the content of speech. Currently, the greatest obstacle to the free discussion of ideas is the fact that special interests can spend unlimited amounts of money on 15-second commercials – sound-bites that drown out serious discussion. The law has not caught up with the obvious fact that, in an age of mass media, moneyed interests are a threat to freedom of speech, because their advertising overwhelms the speech of individuals.

It is possible that the liberal reaction against Citizens United will lead to changes for the better. President Obama condemned the decision, saying that it "gives the special interests and their lobbyists even more power in Washington – while undermining the influence of average Americans who make small contributions to support their preferred candidates."[228] and adding that "this ruling strikes at our democracy itself."[229] The decision led to an upsurge of political activism, both to overturn this decision and to support public financing for election campaigns, which might ultimately reduce the influence of big money in political campaigns.

Chapter 7
The Future of Liberalism

It was inevitable that classical liberalism would be eclipsed by laissez-faire liberalism in the nineteenth century and by modernist liberalism in the twentieth century, times when there was an urgent need for economic growth to overcome scarcity. Laissez-faire liberalism was important when the market economy was the engine of growth. Modernist liberalism was important when the technological economy was the engine of growth.

But now, to move to an era of slower growth, we need to go back to something more like classical liberalism. We need to give people the choice of downshifting economically, so individuals and face-to-face groups can do more for themselves. We need to realize that, because we now have enough, consuming more is less important than having more time to do for ourselves.

The conventional history of liberalism, which traces its roots to the commercial values that promoted economic growth from the seventeenth through the twentieth century, is an obstacle to developing the new version of liberalism needed for the twenty-first century.

Liberalism has a history that began long before laissez faire, and liberalism has a future that extends beyond modernism. The tradition of classical moral liberalism runs from Athens and Rome to Jeffersonian America, to Emerson and Thoreau, to the idealism of Martin Luther King's civil rights movement. Recovering this classical liberal tradition can help us deal with the problems of growth that we will face in the coming century.

Our Conceptual Blind Spot

Some of the policies sketched in the previous chapter seem so obvious that we have to wonder why they have little or no place in the conventional political debate. For example, choice of work hours has been implemented successfully in the Netherlands and Germany. It obviously would let many people make their lives more satisfying by choosing the work-life balance that best suits their circumstances. It obviously would help us deal with environmental problems, such as global warming, by slowing economic growth a bit. Yet not a single American politician is talking about giving us the freedom to make this choice.

We overlook these policies because of fundamental failings of contemporary conservatism and liberalism. Looking at why they are ignored can help us to move beyond the limits of contemporary politics.

The Conservative Blind Spot

Conservatives support some of the individual choices discussed in the previous chapter, such as medical savings accounts, non-discriminatory tax credits for child care, and federal matching funds for voluntary groups, but they often back distorted forms of these policies because they believe in free markets and in commercial values. They back individually purchased health insurance with medical savings accounts, which would not work because it would not create risk pools for people who are hard to insure. They back matching funds for donations of money to charities but not for donations of time to charities, which would give the very rich a disproportionate influence over social policy.

Though they sometimes talk about these other individual choices, conservatives never mention choice of work hours. Choice of work hours clearly should be a part of laissez-faire economic theory: Just as the free market allows people to choose freely among different commodities so they can purchase the combination of products that gives them the most satisfaction, the free market should also allow people to choose freely between more income and more leisure, so they can have the combination that gives them the most satisfaction. This is such an obvious part of free-market theory that laissez-faire liberals such as John Stuart Mill took it for granted.[230] But contemporary conservatives do not mention it because they are really more pro-business than pro-free-market. They will not back a policy that would give employers less control over workers and would slow economic growth, even if free market theory clearly implies that they should.

Because they are primarily pro-business, conservatives have never spent much time working on social policies that allow more choice, though they sometimes mention these policies in their campaigns. For example, the first President Bush talked about non-discriminatory taxes for child care during his campaign, and the second President Bush talked about "compassionate conservatism" and matching funds for charities during his campaign, but neither of them did anything about these issues after they were elected. These ideas are good for appealing to the public, which wants less top-down control and more choices, but they are not important enough to focus on after you are elected.

And because they are primarily pro-business, they will not give people choice of work time, which could provide the free time needed to take advantage of the other choices that conservatives do support. They back tax credits for parents who care for their own children, but they do not talk about giving people the choice of having more time to care for their own children. They back matching funds for voluntary organizations, but they do not talk about giving people the choice of having more time to volunteer at those organizations.

Conservatives' support for individual choice is distorted and incomplete.

Their support for political choice of how we manage the public realm is non-existent, because of their laissez-faire ideology and their commercial values. From off-road vehicles to urban sprawl to global warming, conservatives oppose any political limits on individual choices that damage the public realm.

The Liberal Blind Spot

Liberals support some of the political choices discussed in the previous chapter, but they do not support the individual choices because they still have the old modernist beliefs that most decisions in the modern economy are technical decisions that are beyond the ken of most people, and that we need to set up centralized organizations to provide ordinary people with more services.

Liberals support limits on off-road vehicles in parks, and they realize that this is a political choice about how we want to use the public realm. But this choice is marginal to the economy: It applies to recreational areas that are deliberately kept free of commercial activity.

Liberals also support more walkable neighborhoods, an issue that is importantly economically, but they think that this decision is primarily a technical problem for planners to solve rather than a political choice of how we want to live. There are endless environmental studies showing exactly how much we could reduce greenhouse gas emissions, reduce oil imports, or reduce urban air pollution by building walkable neighborhoods, and these technical studies are cited and used as the basis of city-planning decisions. There is relatively little talk about which is a better way of life, living in walkable cities or living in auto-dependent, and this talk is not used as the basis of city planning decisions.

For example, there have been a few cases where urban automobile use has been limited slightly by the Clean Air Act, but that happens when the planners say that it is necessary to drive less to keep air pollution down to the level that the law requires because scientists have determined that is necessary to protect health. It does not happen because people are making a political choice among the different ways of life that are implied by different levels of automobile use.

Though they support political choices in a limited and incomplete way, liberals do not support the individual choices described in the previous chapter, because they take the old modernist stance that we should set up centralized organizations managed by experts to provide us with social services. Liberals support a federal bureaucracy to provide single-payer health insurance, and they do not support medical savings accounts to let people make choices about their own health care. Liberals support a federal bureaucracy to provide universal preschool, and they do not support non-discriminatory tax credits to give more people the option of caring for their own preschool children. Liberals support federal welfare bureaucracies to help the poor, and they do not support federal matching funds for voluntary groups that help the poor.

Liberals still take the old modernist stance that their role is to demand more money to provide more of these services for their constituents – more spending on health care, more spending on education, more spending on welfare.

Most striking, liberals do not even think about choice of work hours. Instead, they think of "jobs" as a service that the economy provides us: They demand that the government should provide everyone with jobs, just as they demand that the government should provide everyone with health insurance and preschool.

Since the Depression, liberals have demanded that the government stimulate the economy to provide everyone with more standard 40-hour-per-week jobs. They have not thought about letting people choose their own standard of living by deciding whether to work shorter hours, and managing the economy to give people the number of hours that they want. They think they are providing us with a service by stimulating the economy and providing more jobs – so they do not see that they are actually forcing us to do unnecessary work.

Both individual choices and economically important political choices fall into the conceptual blind-spot of modernist liberalism, because these choices let people make serious decisions for themselves. Modernists believe that the serious decisions in our economy are complex, technical decisions that must be made by experts, and ordinary people can only have freedom in a very narrow private realm.

Moral and Political Decisions

We do not see that these choices are possible, because we reduce moral and political decisions about what sort of lives we live to technical problems that the planners should solve for us. We believe that economic planners should provide us with jobs, so we ignore the individual decisions about our work hours that should underlie this economic planning. We believe that urban planners should design livable cities, so we ignore the political decisions about what sort of neighborhoods we want to live in that should underlie this urban planning.

A century ago, it made some sense to give decision-making power to the experts. At the beginning of the twentieth century, most Americans had incomes near the poverty level, and industrialization promised to increase the standard of living dramatically. Because people lacked obvious necessities, it was plausible to give decision-making power to experts who could maximize production. There was no need to ask moral and political questions about what to produce when people lacked decent housing, health care, and education.

It no longer makes sense for the experts to make all the decisions in today's surplus economy.

For example, in 1900, many urban workers lived in tenements where all the families on a floor shared one toilet, where inner rooms had no window, and where there was nowhere for children to play. Urban planners developed schemes for mass produced worker's housing projects that were monotonous and drab but that at least had a private bath for each family, windows in each room, and playgrounds for the children – making them an immense improvement over the tenements. In 2000, when America's per capita income was more than seven times as great as in 1900, most American workers lived in the suburbs. Once they have reached this level of affluence, workers have many reasonable choices for housing, depending on what sort of neighborhood they want to live in: comfortable apartments, row houses, streetcar suburbs, or sprawl suburbs. It no longer makes sense for urban planners to design standardized housing that gives workers the basics of a decent life.

The same is true of other social services. In 1900, most Americans had little or no access to health care, and children had only minimal education in overcrowded schools. At the time, it made sense to talk about providing standardized government health care and to expand the public school system dramatically to provide standardized education. But today, Americans spend more on health care and on education than the other developing nations, but our results are worse than the average. At this level of affluence, we should be able to make choices about our health care and our children's education. It no longer makes sense to say we should focus on spending even more money on centralized organizations to produce even more health care and even more preschools.

Most important, in an affluent economy, people should be able to choose their standard of living. In 1900, when the average person was near the poverty line, it made sense to stimulate the economy and promote growth. In the wake of the Depression, economic planners took on the task of promoting growth that was a rapid as possible, consistent with economic stability.

But today, most Americans already have enough to be economically comfortable, and so we should be able to choose our standard of living. This involves individual choices, such as the choice of work hours, and political choices, such as the choice of whether to build walkable or automobile-dependent cities. In today's economy, the standard of living should be a moral and political decision, a decision about what sort of life we want to live, not a technical problem that the economic planners solve for us.

This is the conceptual blind spot that afflicts our politics. We have not see the choices that affluence has opened for us. We still think in the same way as we did one hundred years ago, during a time of scarcity. Liberal politics has not caught up with this fundamental socio-economic change.

A New Direction

The policies sketched briefly in the previous chapter are not comprehensive, but they do point toward a new direction for liberalism. They move beyond the modernist liberalism of the twentieth century, which tried to help people by stimulating rapid economic growth and using the resulting prosperity to fund centralized bureaucracies that provide services. Instead, they move toward the Jeffersonian values that are the source of American liberalism.

These policies promote decentralization and individual choice. They help low and middle-income people, but instead of funding centralized bureaucracies to provide services, they give this funding to people directly – by making the income tax more progressive, by giving people medical savings accounts, by providing non-discriminatory funding for child care, by providing funding to match the time that people volunteer at community organizations. A great deal of centralization obviously is needed in a modern society, but these policies add a mix of de-centralized elements, to give people more opportunities to make significant decisions about their own lives.

These policies promote positive freedom: They promote individual responsibility in addition to promoting individual choice. Instead of setting up a centralized child-care system, they give child-care funding to parents and expect that parents will take more responsibility for raising their own children. Instead of setting up a centralized health-insurance system, they provide funding that lets people make decisions about their own health care and expect that people will take more responsibility for their own health. Instead of setting up a centralized welfare system, they give matching funds to local groups and expect that people will volunteer in these groups. Instead of promoting economic growth to provide jobs, they give people choice of work hours and expect that people will be able to make good use of their free time.

These policies promote slower economic growth, which is important at a time when economic growth has become a threat to the world's environment. They allow individual choices that let people downshift economically. They let people shorter work hours, so they have more free time rather than more income. They fund services in ways that let people downshift and consume less, giving people the choice of saving money spent on medical care and of staying home to care for their own children. They also allow political choices that would let society as a whole consume less, such as the choice to build walkable cities.

These policies involve a new vision of the future. During the twentieth century, we aimed at a future of endlessly increasing consumption, and we encouraged economic growth that was as rapid as possible. Instead, we need to envision a future where everyone is economically comfortable, and everyone also has enough free time to do for themselves. We have reached a point where most Americans consume more than enough but do not have enough time: Most Americans obviously would benefit from more time to care for their preschool children, more time to spend with their families, more time to exercise, more time to volunteer in their communities.

In addition to these practical steps to improve our lives, in order to develop a new vision of the future, we also need to revive the classical ideal of leisure. In the classical view, leisure is used to develop our humanity as fully as possible, for example, by devoting ourselves to music, athletics, study, arts, and politics. Aristotle said that "we work to have leisure,"[231] because our work consists of activities that are means to an end, while our leisure consists of activities that are ends in themselves, activities that let us develop our talents as fully as possible. Education will always have to focus on vocational skills, but it should also begin to focus on teaching children to make good use of their free time to develop their humanity fully.

Modernizing philosophers have done their best to undermine this classical ideal of the good life. It began in the seventeenth century, when Hobbes said explicitly that his ethics, based on appetites and aversions implies that there is no limit to human desires, unlike classical ethics:

> ...the Felicity of this life, consisteth not in the repose of a mind satisfied. For there is no such *Finis ultimus* (utmost ayme,) nor *Summum Bonum* (greatest Good,) as is spoken of in the books of the old Morall Philosophers. ... Felicity is a continuall progress of the desire, from one object to another....[232]

It continued to the twentieth century, when Dewey rejected classical ethics because "the process of growth, improvement and progress, rather than the static outcome and result, become the significant thing. ... Growth itself is the only moral 'end.'"²³³ But in the twenty-first century, we will need to recognize that ecological limits require a shift away from this continual progress of the desire from one object to another and away from the consumerism and rapid economic growth that it implies.

We have seen that, all through history, positive freedom has only blossomed briefly before being undermined by economic growth. In the past, growth was inevitable: Economic scarcity caused real hardship, so economic growth was urgently needed, even though it undermined positive freedom. But now that we have moved beyond scarcity, and now that growth has become a danger to the environment, the single-minded pursuit of economic growth is no longer inevitable: Once we have enough to be economically comfortable, it makes sense to slow growth in order to give ourselves more positive freedom.

Now, we can make this choice. It no longer needs to be true, as it was when Emerson wrote, that "A terrible machine has possessed itself of the ground, the air, and the men and women, and hardly even thought is free" and that "Things are in the saddle and ride mankind."²³⁴

Now that we consume enough, the most important ways to improve our lives involve doing more for ourselves rather than consuming even more. We already consume enough medical care, and the most important thing we can do to improve our health to exercise and eat good diets. We already consume enough schooling, and the most important thing we can do to improve education is to do a better job of raising our own children. We already consume enough transportation, and the most important thing we can do to make our make our cities livable is to build neighborhoods where people can walk around on their own two feet. We already consume enough in general, and the most important thing we can do to improve the quality of our lives is not to buy a bigger SUV and a bigger McMansion but instead to make good use of our free time to be with our families, to be active in our communities, and to develop our talents.

Because people should take more responsibility for protecting their own health, raising their own children, and making good use of their own free time, we need to create a moral climate that encourages people to act responsibly. That means we must reject the self-interested individualism of laissez-faire and modernist liberalism and return to the moral individualism of classical liberalism.

We have done this in the case of health. Liberals supported policies that convinced people to give up smoking, and they also backed anti-smoking laws to control self-destructive personal behavior. In the case of health, liberals have the moral high ground: When Rush Limbaugh complains about the "food police," it is very obvious that he is the one promoting self-indulgent, self-destructive behavior.

Americans rejected modernist liberalism when it became clear that all the money spent on social programs during 1960s and 1970s did not make up for the declining standards of behavior that liberals seemed to promote, and Americans will support liberalism again when they see it promote higher standards of behavior. Rather than seeing liberals as people who condone family breakdown and want government to take over families responsibilities, they should see liberals as the ones who expect that people do more for their families – who expect people to cut back on their work hours to spend more time with their children. They should also see liberals as people who want us to make a personal effort to live well, and conservatives as people who want us to indulge in endless gluttonous consumerism.

We need to revive the contrast between the two political parties that existed in early America. As we have seen, Alexander Hamilton admitted that Jefferson's Democrats were the party of republican virtue and his Federalists were the party of commercial modernity, which corrupted a nation's character. In the wake of the 1960s, conservatives succeeded in painting modernist liberals as the ones who were undermining our virtues and corrupting the nation's character. If we return to the ideal of classical liberalism, liberals will have the moral high ground once again.

Negative or Positive Freedom

The best known defense of negative freedom is Isaiah Berlin's essay *Two Concepts of Liberty*.[235] Berlin says we should limit ourselves to the modest idea of negative freedom, because the idea of positive freedom can easily be abused to justify totalitarianism. He defines positive freedom as the freedom to be your best self, and he claims that the idea is dangerous because there is no good answer to the question of who should decide what each person's best self is, so authoritarian governments can claim the right to make that decision for everyone.

Berlin was reacting against the Nazis and Communists, who abused the idea of positive freedom in exactly this way, but he did not admit that the idea of negative freedom can also be abused. He does not mention that this idea was abused in the past by laissez faire capitalism.[236] More important, he does not realize that this idea was being abused as he wrote: The modern technological economy was taking over the responsibilities of ordinary people and leaving them powerless, and the idea of negative freedom was being abused to claim that this powerlessness did not make people less free.

Berlin is wrong to say there is no good answer to the question of who should decide what each person's best self is. In the liberal tradition, people should decide this question for themselves. The idea of positive freedom, as it is defined by classical liberalism, cannot be abused to justify an authoritarian state, because it centers on freedom of conscience in the broadest sense of that term. According to classical liberalism, freedom is the right to perform what you believe are your obligations, which implies that you must make the decisions about what are your obligations.

Negative freedom protects trivial personal behavior. Laws against loitering or smoking in public places limit negative freedom, the laissez-faire and modernist liberal idea that we have the right to do what we please as long as it does not hurt someone else. They do not limit positive freedom, the classical liberal idea that we have rights based on what we believe are our moral obligations. No one believes that he has a moral obligation to loiter or to smoke cigarettes.

The classical idea of positive freedom protects our right to do things important enough that we feel we have an obligation to do them, such as raising our children and deciding what sort of cities we want to live in.

Today, we have reached a point where the idea of negative freedom is the real threat to the future of liberalism, because it has been carried so far that it degrades the idea of freedom. Writers who would have been liberals a few decades ago have moved to the center, by becoming civic republicans or communitarians. They have reacted so strongly against the failures of negative freedom that they falter in the defense of positive freedom.

For example, our best known civic republican writer, Michael Sandel, reserves some of his harshest criticism for the Supreme Court decision that gave Jehovah's Witnesses the right to refuse to salute the flag in the public schools,[237] claiming that this ceremony helps form the common values needed for republican self-government. They might have agreed with Sandel in the republic of Florence, but they would have condemned him after republicanism fused with radical Protestantism in England and America, creating our ideal of freedom of religion. John Milton despised above all things the "forcing of conscience"[238] – requiring people to take part in ceremonies they do not believe in – and he would have been disgusted by laws requiring Jehovah's Witnesses to violate their religious beliefs by saluting the flag. Established churches that people were compelled to attend were common in Europe at the time of the American revolution, and the founders obviously had these sorts of compulsory ceremonies in mind when they wrote the First Amendment.

Likewise, the well known communitarian writer, Mary Ann Glendon, argues for laws banning pornography on the grounds that we have to balance free speech against the needs of the community.[239] But this argument is dangerous to real freedom of speech. It could also be used by right-wingers who want to ban books about evolution or by left-wingers who want to ban speech that offends minorities; these people also believe that the right to free speech should be balanced against the needs of the community.

Glendon's defense of free speech is shaky, because she takes for granted the negative idea of freedom: If free speech means the right to say anything you want without government interference, then it obviously has to be balanced against the needs of the community, not only to restrict pornography but also to stop commercial fraud and to stop people from yelling "fire" in a crowded theater as a prank. But freedom of speech is safe from this sort of balancing if we base it on the positive idea of freedom: Because people have an obligation to the truth, they have an absolute right to advocate ideas they believe are true. This positive idea of free speech does not protect pornography or fraud. It leaves room for limiting the time or manner of speech: We can have laws limiting noise levels or limiting speech when there is a clear and present danger of causing a riot. But it means that people have an absolute right to advocate ideas, however unpopular, offensive, or dangerous they are. When the right tries to ban the teaching of evolution, or when the left tries to ban speech that offends minorities, they are balancing free speech against what they believe to be the welfare of the community, and classical liberals would respond that people have a right to advocate ideas they believe are true, even if these ideas are offensive or threatening to the community.

Civic republicans and communitarians criticize liberals for their individualism, and they want to promote common values to balance this individualism – but they are reacting against the self-interested individualism of modernist liberalism, and they fail to see that the moral individualism of classical liberalism has a very different effect on national character. People who demand the right to sell pornography or to loiter on street corners are very different from people who advocate unpopular ideas because they believe in them, and are certainly very different from people like the Jehovah's Witnesses, who insist on following their religious obligations in the face of persecution.

Thomas Jefferson believed that people would develop civic virtue by managing their own farms or businesses, raising their own children, and participating in the government of their own communities. They would develop the character they needed to be citizens of a republic by running their own lives in these small ways – not by having government compel them to join in a ritual pledge of allegiance to the flag.

Of course, we cannot go back to Jefferson's America of economically independent family farms, small family businesses, and small-town government, but we can adapt the classical liberal ideal of positive freedom to modern conditions. We can reject the modernist focus on centralized bureaucracies that provide services to passive consumers, and instead look for social policies that promote positive freedom.

These policies would let people make more decisions for themselves, individual decisions about their own health care, about their own child care, and about their own work hours, as well as political decisions about the public realm in their own neighborhoods. These policies would strengthen civil society by promoting voluntary associations and local government. These policies would give people the opportunity to downshift economically, so they have free time to raise their own children, to be active in their own communities, and to fully develop their own humanity.

Notes

1. To give just one example, when Mary Ann Glendon describes the political philosophy that "inspired the American founders," she says that "natural rights theories were elaborated for us principally by Hobbes and Locke." Mary Ann Glendon, *Rights Talk: The Impoverishment of Political Discourse* (New York, The Free Press, 1991) p. 13.

2. For example, see the introduction to Alan Brinkley, *The End of Reform, New Deal Liberalism in Recession and War* (New York, Vintage, 1995). Brinkley says that laissez-faire liberalism was followed by two distinct phases of modern liberalism, a genuinely reformist movement from early in the century through the early New Deal, followed by a movement dedicated to propping up the status quo during the late New Deal and postwar period. But he admits that those early ideas did not really add up to a coherent theory of liberalism, and I think it makes more sense to see them as a period of confusion as liberalism moved from the certainties of the nineteenth century to the certainties of the postwar period.

3. The word "liberal" was first used to refer to politics and theology that were the opposite of conservative in Britain during the 1820s. At the time, this was the name of a radical political faction in France, and English Tories used the word to refer to the more advanced faction of the Whigs, implying that they were no different from French radicals. Because the word "liberal" was already used in a complimentary sense in English, the advanced Whigs began to call themselves liberals. Bentham and Mill used the word liberal as the opposite of conservative, and the terms

"liberal" and "conservative" became common currency in England during the debate over the Reform Act of 1832. Yet these terms were not as common in America at the time: for example, in his "Lecture on the Times," delivered in 1841, Emerson says that the two great political movements are "conservatism" and "reform" – not conservatism and liberalism.

The British political parties came to be called Conservative and Liberal rather than Tory and Whig because of a party realignment that began when the Whigs joined with the Radicals in 1830. Robert Peel defeated this alliance and became Prime Minister in 1841, by putting together a new coalition of Tories and conservative Whigs, to form the new Conservative party, and the remaining coalition of advanced Whigs and Radicals were generally called the Liberal Party. Perhaps the new party names in Britain gave the terms "liberal" and "conservative" the high profile that made Americans adopt these terms also.

4. Isaiah Berlin's *Two Concepts of Liberty* is the best known essay on positive and negative freedom, but Berlin borrowed the terms from the nineteenth-century British neo-Hegelian T.H. Green. Green is discussed in Chapter 3, and Berlin's essay is discussed in Chapter 7.

5. Michael Sandel, *Democracy's Discontent* (Cambridge, Mass., The Belknap Press of Harvard University Press, 1996) p. 1.

6. Health care is discussed in more detail in Chapter 6.

7. In Egypt in Ptolemaic times, for example, there were over two hundred taxes, including a sales tax, a tax on home rents, an inheritance tax, and a poll tax, and the wealthy were also obligated to give donations to the monarchy and priests. In addition, there were tariffs on goods at the borders of the empire and also at the borders of each of its provinces, and there were royal monopolies in oil, papyrus, textiles, mining, and banking.

8. Hesiod begins the poem by describing the small farmers who want to get rich: "A man grows eager, seeing another rich / From ploughing, planting, ordering his house; / So neighbor vies with neighbor in the rush / For wealth: this strife is good for mortal men..." Dorathea Wender, trans., Hesiod, *Theogony, Works and Days*, Theognis, *Elegies* (Harmondsworth, Middlesex, England: Penguin Books, 1973) p. 59. Sometimes Hesiod's advice about scrimping and saving sounds like it could come from Benjamin Franklin: "Even if your supply / Is small, and if you add a little bit, / And do it often, soon it will be big." *ibid.* p. 70.

9. *From Plutarch's Lives*, Edward C. Lindeman, ed, (New York, New American Library: Mentor Books, 1950) "Lycurgus" on pp. 11-37.

10. This equality had broken down by Aristotle's time, as he says: "...some Spartans have far too much property, others very little indeed; the land has come into the possession of a small number.... For their lawgiver, while he quite rightly did not approve of buying and selling existing estates, left it open to anyone to transfer land to other ownership by gift; and this of course leads to the same result." *Politics*, II, 9, A. Sinclair trans. (Baltimore, Maryland, Penguin Books, 1962) p. 86. By Aristotle's time, some of the Spartans were living in a way that was far from what we call Spartan: "at Sparta, women live without restraint, enjoying every license and indulging in every luxury. One inevitable result of such a way of life is that great importance is attached to being rich...." *ibid.*, p. 85.

11. Alfred Zimmern, *The Greek Commonwealth: Politics and Economics in Fifth-Century Athens* (Oxford: Clarendon Press, 1931) pp. 174-178.

12. Xenophon wrote that the thirty killed more people during the eight months that they were in power than the Spartans had killed in ten years of war. Xenophon, *History of Greece*, II, 4, 21.

13. Thucidides, *The Peloponnesian War*, II, 37, trans. Rex Warner (NY, Penguin Books, 1954) p. 145.

14. Most of the second book of the *Politics* is a criticism of Plato's *Republic*. It says: "certainly there must be some unity in a state, as in a household, but not an absolutely total unity. There comes a point when the effect of unification is that the state, if it does not cease to be a state altogether, will certainly be a very much worse one; it is as if one were to reduce harmony to unison or rhythm to a single beat. As we have said before, a city must be a plurality, depending on education for its common unity. And it is very strange that Plato, whose intention it was to introduce an education which he believed would make the city good, should think he could obtain good results by such methods. It is going the wrong way about it; regulations about property are no substitute for the training of the character and the intellect or for using the laws and customs of the community to that end." Aristotle, *Politics* II, 5, T. A. Sinclair trans. (Baltimore, Maryland, Penguin Books, 1962) p. 65.

15. Aristotle writes about "...the old hints for the preservation of tyranny, such as 'Cut off the tops and get rid of men of independent views,' and 'Don't allow getting together in clubs for social and cultural activities or anything of that kind; these are the breeding grounds of independence and self-confidence, two things which a tyrant must guard against,' and 'Do not allow schools or other institutions where men pursue learning together, and generally ensure that people do not get to know each other well, for that establishes mutual confidence.' Another piece of traditional advice to a tyrant tells him to keep the dwellers in the city always within his view and require them to spend much time at his palace gates; their activities then will not be kept secret and by constantly performing servile obligations they will become used to having no minds of their own. There are other precepts of the same kind and having the same purpose

among the Persians and other foreign monarchies. Similarly, a tyrant should endeavor to keep himself aware of everything that is said or done among his subjects; he should have spies ...." *Politics* V, 11, Sinclair p. 65.

16. "...inequality is generally at the bottom of internal warfare in states. ... a constitution of the middle classes is nearer to 'that of the people' than to 'that of the few', and is of all such constitutions the most reliable." *Politics*, V, 1, Sinclair, p. 191-192.

17. "There are three elements in all constitutions [polities], and every serious lawgiver must look for the best set-up in each of the three.... The three elements are, first, the deliberative, discussion about everything of national importance, second, the executive, the whole complex of officials and authorities, their number and nature, the limits of their powers, and the methods by which they are selected, and third, the judicial system. The powers of the deliberative or policy-making element cover decisions as to war and peace, the making and dissolving of alliances, legislation, the penalties of death, exile and confiscation of goods, the election of officials, and the investigation of their conduct during their tenure." *Politics* IV, 14, Sinclair p. 179. The deliberative branch passes legislation but has more powers than a purely legislative branch would, such as the power of selecting officials; Aristotle was thinking of Athens' Assembly, which would naturally elect officials when it met to pass laws, because it included all citizens. Note that, when Aristotle says "all constitutions" must have these features, he does not mean all governments, only constitutional governments based on law. He believed the Athenian democracy of his time was not a constitutional government, because it ignored the law, particularly because it ignored the division of powers between the branches of government, as he says: "[Demagogues] bring every question before the popular assembly, whose decrees can supersede the written law. ... when

people object to the exercise of authority by officials, on the ground that the authority belongs to the people, the demagogue seizes on this an excuse for abolishing the office. So if you were to say that such a democracy is not a constitution at all, you would in my opinion be perfectly right. Where laws do not rule, there is no constitution." *Politics* IV, 4, Sinclair p. 160-161. There are obvious opportunities for abuse, because Aristotle assumed that the deliberative branch would be like the Athenian *Ecclesia* of his day, the body of all citizens that passed legislation and elected officials. It took two millennia for political philosophy (beginning with Montesquieu) to take the obvious next step and replace Aristotle's deliberative, executive and judicial branches of government with our familiar legislative, executive, and judicial branches, strengthening the separation of powers by making the executive independent of the legislature.

18. Aristotle discusses a number of ways to balance the power of the oligarchic upper house and the democratic lower house and finally settles on this one: "In the constitutions which are truly polities ... the smaller body has an absolute right of veto, but not of giving a final decision in any other sense; the matter is then always referred to the larger body." *Politics* IV, 14, Sinclair p. 182. But it seems that he would be satisfied with any of the mechanisms he suggests, as long as they give both classes a voice and do not let one run roughshod over another. He also suggests other ways of reducing the influence of the people, such as not giving salaries to government officials, so only the rich can serve. (*Politics* V, 8, Sinclair p. 212) and setting the property qualification for citizenship high enough to exclude as many people as possible without actually making citizens a minority of the city's residents (*Politics* IV, 13, Sinclair p. 177).

19. *Politics* I, 2, Sinclair p. 26-27.

20. "So any piece of property can be regarded as a tool enabling a man to live; and his property is an assemblage of such tools,

including his slaves …. For suppose that every tool we had could perform its function, either at our bidding or itself perceiving the need, like the statues made by Daedelus or the wheeled tripods of Hephaestus, of which the poet says that 'self-moved they enter the assembly of the gods' – and suppose that the shuttles in a loom could fly to and fro and a plucker play on a lyre all self-moved, then manufacturers would have no need of workers nor masters of slaves." *Politics* I, 13, Sinclair p. 31.

21. *Politics* VII, 9, Sinclair p. 273.

22. For a collection of the most important fragments that summarize stoic thinking on ethics, see A. A. Long and D.N. Sedley, *The Hellenistic Philosophers, vol. 1: Translations of the Principal Sources with Philosophical Commentary* (New York and Cambridge, Cambridge University Press, 1987) pp. 344-437.

23. A few stoics did write on political philosophy. The *Republic* of Zeno, the founder of stoicism (who was born in 334 BC, just after Philip of Macedon conquered Greece) was the most famous book on politics by a stoic; from the few fragments that survive, we can see that it attacked contemporary institutions and values – for example, it condemned the conventional educational curriculum, called for a community of wives, and said that men and women should wear the same clothing. Zeno was trying to describe a way of life that was based on reason, not convention; because these rational moral laws apply to all people, he used them as the basis of his ideal state. Chrysippus, the third leader of the stoic school, also wrote a *Republic*, and surviving fragments call for incest and cannibalism; like Zeno, he was using political theory to attack conventional morality and support morality based on reason, rather than trying to devise a political order that allows moral autonomy. See Long & Sedley, pp. 429-437. The historian Polybius was another stoic whose political ideas were important historically. A Greek living and writing in Rome at the time that the Roman republic was conquering Greece, Polybius used

Aristotle's idea of a mixed system to try to understand why empires rise and fall, arguing that because a constitution could never be perfectly balanced, it must ultimately became corrupt and unstable. His history was influential in bringing Aristotle's ideas to the Florentine Civic Humanists, who tried to devise a more perfectly balanced mixed system. See J.G.A. Pocock, *The Machiavellian Moment: Florentine Political Thought and the Atlantic Republican Tradition* (Princeton, N. J., Princeton University Press, 1975) p. 79-80. Panaetius, a later Greek stoic, wrote a book about politics that may have influenced Cicero; since one of his books about ethics, *On Appropriate Actions*, was the model for Cicero's *On Duties*, it seems plausible that he also influenced Cicero's views about politics. Panaetius was part of the group of Greek philosophers that formed around Scipio Africanus the younger, who was instrumental in bringing Greek thought to Rome, and Scipio took him on an embassy to Egypt in 140 BC. Posodonius, a pupil of Panaetius, wrote a history of Rome that began where Polybius had left off: surviving fragments show that he believed in aristocratic rule but feared that moral decay was causing the Romans to lose their dominance. It is striking that the stoics who wrote about politics included the early stoics, Zeno and Chrysippus, who wrote about ideal states to criticize the conventional morality of their time rather than because they wanted political change, and Polybius, Panaetius and Posodonius, who were really concerned about what was a good state because they had extensive contact with the Roman republic. Most stoics lived under empires, and there was no reason for them to speculate on what sort of state would make people happiest or promote moral autonomy: They had no hope of changing society; they believed that virtue was the only good and that you could practice virtue regardless of your external situation.

24. Cicero, *De Finibus Bonurum et Malorum (Of Ends)*, V, 20, 57, trans. H. Rackham, (Cambridge, Mass., and London, Harvard

University and William Heineman: Loeb Classical Library, 1931) p. 459.

25. Cicero, *Laws*, III, 19, in *De Republica and De Legibus*, trans. C.W. Keyes (Cambridge, Mass., and London, Harvard University and William Heineman: Loeb Classical Library, 1928) p. 511.

26. Cicero, *Laws*, III, 19, p. 511.

27. Cicero, *Laws*, III, 2, p. 461.

28. Cicero, *Laws*, III, 15, p. 499.

29. Cicero, *Laws*, III, 17, p. 505.

30. When he describes possible types of government, Aristotle says that a polity is a government where all citizens govern for the common good while a democracy is a government where the many govern for their own self-interest (just as an aristocracy is a government where the few govern for the common good while an oligarchy is a government where the few govern for their own self-interest, and a monarchy is a government where one governs for the common good while a tyranny is a government where one governs for his own self-interest). Throughout the *Politics*, he usually uses the word democracy to mean a government where the many ignore the law for the sake of their self-interest. But when he is listing all the possible types of democracy, he says that the word is most truly used to refer to a democracy where there is a rule of law: "The first, and most truly so called, variety of democracy is that which is based on the principle of equality. In such, the law lays down that the poor shall not enjoy any advantage over the rich, that neither class shall dominate the other but both shall be exactly similar." *Politics* IV, 4, Sinclair p. 159. He adds that democracy declines to the lowest level when "the people is sovereign and not the law. This occurs when the will of the people, expressed in decrees or resolutions, can overrule the provisions of the law. It is the popular political leaders, the demagogues, that bring about this state of affairs.

When states are democratically governed according to law, there are no demagogues; the best citizens are securely in the saddle; but where the laws are not sovereign, there you find demagogues." *Politics* IV, 4, Sinclair p. 160.

31. "... if, as is generally held, freedom is especially to be found in democracy, and also equality, this condition is best realized when all share in equal measure the whole *politeia*." *Politics* IV, 4, Sinclair p. 159.

32. According to the legend, Whittington came to London as a boy, worked as a scullion, and sold his cat to a rat infested ship. As he was leaving the city to escape the rough treatment in the kitchen where he worked, he heard the ringing bells of Saint Mary-le-Bow church saying to him: "Turn again, Whittington, Lord Mayor of London." He returned to the city, used the money he got by selling his cat to establish himself as a textile merchant, and became so wealthy that he was elected Lord Mayor in 1397, 1406, and 1419, and loaned money to Henry IV and Henry V. Little is known of Whittington's actual childhood, except that he was the son a knight, but the fact that people believed this legend shows that they considered social mobility to be possible and that they admired people who worked their way up from poverty.

33. For example, in 1106, Florence invited all the peasants in the surrounding villages to come there and live as free men. Bologna and other towns paid feudal lords to let their serfs move to the city.

34. Jacques Barzun, *From Dawn to Decadence: 500 Years of Western Cultural Life* (New York, HarperCollins, 2002) p. 93, 97, 107.

35. J.G.A. Pocock, *The Machiavellian Moment: Florentine Political Thought and the Atlantic Republican Tradition* (Princeton, N. J., Princeton University Press, 1975) p. 86.

36. Cited in Stuart Ewen, *All Consuming Images* (New York, Basic Books, 1988) p. 30.

37. Christopher Hill, *The Century of Revolution: 1603-1714* (New York, W.W. Norton & Co., 1980) pp. 30-33.

38. Augustine, *The City of God*, II, 19.

39. Pocock, *The Machiavellian Moment*, pp. 86-88.

40. Pocock, *The Machiavellian Moment*, p. 126 and pp. 209-230, particularly p. 226.

41. For example, when a new Florentine republic began operating in 1495, it abolished all taxes except a 10 percent tax on income from real property. The merchants who dominated the government decided that the old land-owning aristocracy should pay all the taxes! In a sign of how influential the *popolo* still were, however, this government (at the urging of Savonarola) also established a state loan office lending at 5 to 7 percent interest, so the poor did not have to go to private money lenders who charged up to 30 percent. As Pocock says, "At Florence, there really was a popolo . . . with a long tradition of active citizenship, which it would be hard to leave out of account in any theoretical or actual distribution of power." Pocock, *The Machiavellian Moment*, p. 101.

42. J.G.A. Pocock, *The Machiavellian Moment*.

43. "...if a given community has the right to appoint a ruler it is not unjust for the community to depose the king or restrict his power if he abuses it by becoming a tyrant. The community should not be accused of disloyalty if it deposes a tyrant even if it had previously agreed to obey him forever, since he did not rule the community as the office of king requires and thus he deserved to have his subjects break their agreement." On Kingship, Chapter 6, in Paul E. Sigmund, ed., *St. Thomas Aquinas on Politics and Ethics* (New York, Norton, 1988) p. 24.

44. "Here are the sentiments of the most celebrated of all the Guelphic writers: – 'A King who is unfaithful to his duty forfeits his claim to obedience. It is not rebellion to depose him, for he is himself a rebel whom the nation has a right to put down. But it is better to abridge his power, that he may be unable to abuse it. For this purpose, the whole nation ought to have a share in governing itself, the constitution ought to combine a limited and elective monarchy, with an aristocracy of merit, and such an admixture of democracy as shall admit all classes to office, by popular election. No government has a right to levy taxes beyond the limit determined by the people. All political authority is derived from popular suffrage, and all laws must be made by the people or their representatives. There is no security for us as long as we depend on the will of another man.' This language, which contains the earliest exposition of the Whig theory of the revolution, is taken from the works of St. Thomas Aquinas...." Lord Acton, *The History of Freedom*, with an introduction by James C. Holland (Grand Rapids, Michigan, The Acton Institute, 1993) p. 64.

45. Pocock, *The Machiavellian Moment*, p. 396-7.

46. James Harrington, *A System of Politics*, VI, 9, in Charles Blitzer, ed, *The Political Writings of James Harrington* (Indianapolis, Library of Liberal Arts, 1955) p. 19.

47. James Harrington, *The Commonwealth of Oceana*, in Blitzer, p. 56-58.

48. A commonwealth must consist "of the senate debating and proposing, of the people resolving, and of the magistracy executing." *The Commonwealth of Oceana* in Blitzer, p. 77.

49. "... the magistracy ... is different in different commonwealths, but there is one condition that must be the same in every one or it dissolves the commonwealth where it is wanting. And this is no less than that as the hand of the magistrate is the executive

power of the law, so the head of the magistrate is answerable to the people that his execution be according to the law, by which Hobbes may see that the hand or sword that executes the law is in it and not above it." *The Commonwealth of Oceana* in Blitzer, p. 61.

50. "The man that cannot live upon his own must be a servant; but he that can live upon his own may be a freeman. Where a people cannot live upon their own, the government is either monarchy or aristocracy; where a people can live upon their own, the government may be democracy." *A System of Politics*, I, 13-14, in Blitzer, p. 4. See also *The Commonwealth of Oceana*, in Blitzer, pp. 44-45.

51. *The Commonwealth of Oceana*, in Blitzer, p. 37.

52. *The Commonwealth of Oceana*, in Blitzer, p. 115-116.

53. Harrington defined freedom of conscience as the right to worship as you choose without being denied "preferment or employment in the state." *A System of Government*, VI, 3, in Blitzer, p. 18. A national religion is not coercive if it gives people this right. In a sign that he is looking for a compromise that will heal divisions, Harrington concludes that a democracy should have "a council for the equal maintenance both of the national religion and of freedom of conscience...." *A System of Government*, VI, 31, in Blitzer, p. 21. In this concluding statement, a national religion is opposed to freedom of conscience, and the government must balance the two.

54. Under the proper constitution, "nobility ... that ... live upon their own revenues in plenty without engagement either to the tilling of their lands or to other work for their livelihood ... are not only safe but necessary to the natural mixture of a well-ordered commonwealth. For how else can you have a commonwealth that is not entirely mechanical? Or what comparison is there of such commonwealths as are or come nearest

to mechanical (for example, Athens, Switzerland, Holland) to Sparta, Rome, and Venice, plumed with their aristocracies?" (By "mechanical," Harrington means composed of mechanics, that is of manual workers.) *The Commonwealth of Oceana*, in Blitzer, p. 135.

55. He wrote that agriculture would always be the main source of wealth, except "in such cities as subsist most by trade and have little or no land, as Holland and Genoa," *The Commonwealth of Oceana*, in Blitzer, p. 46.

56. Harrington believed there should be a three year term limit, which would give everyone the opportunity to be part of government in the small state that he envisioned and would also prevent politicians from abusing their power: "A popular assembly, rightly ordered, brings up everyone in his turn to give the result of the whole people. If the popular assembly consists of one thousand or more, annually changeable in one-third part by new elections . . . it is rightly ordered...." *A System of Politics*, V, 24-25, in Blitzer, p. 16. "The interval in which a man may administer government for the good of it and not attempt upon it to the harm of it is the fittest term of baring magistracy; and three years in a magistracy described by the law ... is a term in which he cannot attempt upon his government for the hurt of it, but may administer for the good of it...." *A System of Politics*, V, 13, in Blitzer, pp. 13-14.

57. For example, in 1776, a speaker delivering an oration at the grave of one of the heroes of Bunker Hill said "Like Harrington he wrote – like Cicero he spoke – like Hampden he lived – like Wolfe he died," including Harrington in a list of names that everyone would recognize. Blitzer, p. xii.

58. Blitzer, p. xi.

59. Sophocles, *Antigone*, Elizabeth Wyckoff, trans., in David Grene and Richmond Lattimore, ed., *The Complete Greek*

Tragedies (Chicago, University of Chicago Press, 1959) vol. 2, pp. 159-204. Quotations are from lines 453-5, 665-667, and 243-4.

60. Protagoras makes his argument in Plato's *Protagoras*, Thrasymachus makes his in Plato's *Republic*, and Callicles makes his in Plato's *Gorgias*. For a general discussion of these thinkers, see W.K.C. Guthrie, *The Sophists* (Cambridge, Cambridge University Press, 1971).

61. When he was young, Socrates studied natural science, but then he decided to devote himself to the most urgent practical question, what is a good life. He still had a reputation as a natural scientist when he was older. Aristophanes' *The Clouds* satirizes his scientific equipment and reasoning, and in *The Apology*, he has to defend himself against the charge that he believes the sun is a ball of fire rather than a god, saying; he says that he abandoned natural science at an early age in favor of moral philosophy. He used the same rational, critical method to study ethics that scientists used to study nature.

62. For more on Socrates' method, see Gregory Vlastos, *Socrates: Ironist and Moral Philosopher* (Ithaca, NY, Cornell University Press, 1991), particularly pp. 21-44.

63. In the *Apology*, which is one of Plato's earliest dialogs and is closest to Socrates' actual opinions, Socrates emphasizes that he knows nothing and that he is wiser than other people only because they think wrongly that they know something. But even as he protests his total ignorance, he claims knowledge of ethics: "And if I were to claim to be at all wiser than the others, it would be because, not knowing very much about the other world, I do not think I know. But I do know very well that it is evil and disgraceful to do an unjust act...." *Apology*, 29, in Robert D. Cumming, ed., *Euthyphro, Apology, Crito, Phaedo* (Indianapolis, Bobbs-Merrill: Library of Liberal Arts, 1956) p. 35.

64. Cicero, *Republic*, III, 22, in *De Republica and De Legibus*, trans. C.W. Keyes (Cambridge, Mass., and London, Harvard University and William Heineman: Loeb Classical Library, 1928) p. 211. Cicero is stating a common principle of Roman law, that the positive law of the state should conform to natural law. This principle dates back to the third century BC, when Rome began appointing special praetors to deal with cases involving foreigners in the city. Because foreigners had a wide variety of customs, these praetors had been forced to invent the idea of the *ius gentium*, the law common to all nations, which involved basic principles of fair dealing. The circle that gathered around Scipio in the mid-second century BC, to study Greek philosophy and Roman law, identified this *ius gentium* with the *ius naturalis*, the natural law of the Greek stoics, and the two terms were used as synonyms in later Roman legal theory. This led Roman lawyers to argue that the positive law of the state should conform to the natural law. In fact, the main speaker in Cicero's *Republic*, which is written in dialog form, is Scipio. See the translators' introduction to George Holland Sabine and Stanley Barney Smith, translators, Cicero, *On the Commonwealth* (Indianapolis, Bobbs-Merrill/Library of Liberal Arts, 1976) p. 36. As Cicero states the principle in this quotation, though, it does not only mean that the positive law should conform to the natural law: When he says that we need no expounder of the law but ourselves and that the Senate or people (=Assembly) cannot free us from it, he clearly implies that we have an obligation to disobey laws passed by the Senate and Assembly if they conflict with the natural law known to our reason.

65. *Summa* I-II, 96, 4 in St. Thomas Aquinas, *Treatise on Law* (Chicago, Regnery, undated) p. 96-97.

66. A. P. d'Entreves, *Natural Law* (London, Hutchinson University Library, 1970) p. 61.

67. Harrington, *A System of Politics*, VI, 5, in Blitzer, p. 19.

68. John Milton, "Areopagitica" in *The Works of John Milton*, vol. IV, Frank Allen Patterson *et al.*, ed., (New York, Columbia University Press, 1931) p. 319.

69. The initial funded debt of 1697 was 1,200,000 pounds, loaned at the relatively low interest rate of 8 percent, but by 1714, 28,000,000 pounds of the 36,000,000 pounds that the government owed was made up of this sort of funded debt. Incidentally, this was also the first government to engineer a bail-out for investors. The government had given the South Seas Company a monopoly on English trade with Spanish colonies in America, and the price of its stock was driven up by speculators until the bubble burst and prices collapsed; in 1721, Robert Walpole, as first lord of the treasury, convinced the Bank of England to absorb the company's debts. Arthur Birnie, *An Economic History of the British Isles* (London, Methuen & Co.: University Paperbacks, 1961) pp. 188-191.

70. Sandel, *Democracy's Discontent*, p. 142.

71. Cited in Sandel, *Democracy's Discontent*, p. 138.

72. Pocock, *The Machiavellian Moment*, 529.

73. Pocock, *The Machiavellian Moment*, 530.

74. Cited in Arthur M. Schlesinger, Jr., *The Age of Jackson* (New York, New American Library/Mentor Books, 1949) p. 7.

75. Cited in Sandel, *Democracy's Discontent*, p. 135.

76. Cited in Sandel, *Democracy's Discontent*, p. 148.

77. Cited in Sandel, *Democracy's Discontent*, p. 149.

78. Cited in Schlesinger, *The Age of Jackson*, p. 52.

79. Schlesinger, *The Age of Jackson*, p. 73.

80. The Populists were the last political movement to focus on the monetary issues that were so important in the early American republic, and they backed soft money: They followed the policies of Jackson's western supporters, who wanted easy money that created prosperity for themselves rather than for eastern bankers, not the policies of Jackson's eastern supporters and of Jefferson, who wanted tight money to slow industrialization.

81. This section deliberately uses male pronouns and terms (such as "economic man") rather than gender-neutral language, because at the time only men were supposed to work in the market economy. These theories assumed that, in the state of nature (as in the market economy in contemporary England), men pursued their economic self-interest as heads of families, but people did not act out of economic self-interest within their families. Self-interest dominated only the market economy, which was the realm of men.

82. cited in A. P. d'Entreves, *Natural Law*, p. 61.

83. Thomas Hobbes, *Leviathan*, II, 18: "Of the Rights of Sovereigns by Institution."

84. Hobbes, *Leviathan*, II, 21, "Of the Liberty of Subjects."

85. Hobbes, *Leviathan*, II, 21, "Of the Liberty of Subjects."

86. Hobbes does list laws of nature, but he adds that "These dictates of reason, men use to call by the name of laws, but improperly; for they are but conclusions, or theorems concerning what conduceth to the conservation and defense of themselves...." *Leviathan*, I, 15, "Of other Lawes of Nature." Self-preservation is a law of nature in the sense that it describes the actual behavior of living creatures, and Hobbes' "natural laws" are means to self-preservation. His theory of "natural law" does not imply that right or justice exist in nature.

87. Because Hobbes is sometimes called the first modern political philosopher, it is worth pointing out that there were also philosophers in ancient times who believed in social contract theory, hedonism and materialism; Hobbes did not invent these foundational ideas of modern political philosophy. The first statement of social contract theory was in Plato's *Republic*, where Glaucon says that most people believe the following: "when people have both done and suffered injustice and have had experience of both, not being able to avoid the one and obtain the other, they think that they had better agree among themselves to have neither; hence there arise laws, and mutual covenants; and that which is ordained by law is termed by them lawful and just. This they affirm to be the origin and nature of justice...." (*Republic*, II, 358-359, Jowett translation). The Epicureans included social contract theory, hedonism, and materialism among their "key doctrines." Though little social contract theory survives from ancient times, nothing in the writing that we do have suggests that these ideas were meant to expand liberty, and they did not contribute historically to the liberal tradition. The Epicureans concluded, logically enough, that their ideas implied that laws were justified when they increased the amount of pleasure or reduced the amount of pain in the world, without giving us any clear sense of whether this would mean more or less freedom than the norm of their time. Epicurus states the pure social contract theory of justice very clearly in *Key Doctrines* 32-35: "There is no such thing as justice or injustice among those beasts that cannot make agreements not to injure or be injured. This is also true of those tribes that are unable or unwilling to make agreements not to injure or be injured. There is no such thing as justice in the abstract; it is merely a compact between men in their various relations with each other, in whatever circumstances they may be, that they will neither injure nor be injured. Injustice is not evil in itself, but only in the fear and apprehension that one will not escape those

who have been set up to punish the offense." Epicurus, *Letters, Principal Doctrines, and Vatican Sayings*, Russell M. Geer trans. (New York and London, Library of Liberal Arts, 1985) pp. 63-64. See Long and Sedley, *The Hellenistic Philosophers*, pp. 125-139 for an overview of Epicurean social contract theory.

88. "But though Men, when they enter into Society, give up the Equality, Liberty, and Executive Power they had in the State of Nature, into the hands of the Society, to be so far disposed of by the Legislative, as the good of the Society shall require; yet it being only with an intention in every one the better to preserve himself his Liberty and Property ... the power of the Society or Legislative constituted by them can never be suppos'd to extend farther than the common good; but is obliged to secure every ones Property by providing those three defects above-mentioned that made the State of Nature so unsafe and uneasy." John Locke, *Two Treatises of Government*, Peter Laslett, ed. (New York, New American Library: Mentor Books, 1965) p. 398.

89. *Ibid.*, p. 460 *et seq.*

90. "Whatsoever then he removes out of the state that Nature has provided ... he hath mixed his *Labour* with, and joyned to it something that is his own, and thereby makes it his *Property*." John Locke, *Two Treatises of Government*, Section 27 of second treatise (New York, New American Library: Mentor Book, 1963) p. 329.

91. Locke, *Two Treatises*, section 123 of second treatise, p. 395.

92. Locke argues for freedom of religion in *A Letter Concerning Toleration*, on the grounds that government is concerned only with protecting men's "Civil Interests," that is, their "Life, Liberty, Health, and Indolency of Body; and the Possession of outward things, such as Money, Lands, Houses, Furniture, and the like." John Locke, *A Letter Concerning Toleration* (Indianapolis, Hackett Publishing, 1983) p. 26. By contrast, a

church is "a voluntary Society of Men, joining themselves together of their own accord in order to the publick worshipping of God in such manner as they judge acceptable to Him and effectual to the Salvation of their Souls." p. 28. Thus, "the Church it self is a thing absolutely separate and distinct from the commonwealth. The Boundaries on both sides are fixed and immovable. He jumbles Heaven and Earth together, the things most remote and opposite, who mixes these two Societies, which are in their Original, End, Business, and in every thing perfectly distinct and infinitely different from each other." p. 33. In other words, Locke believed that we should be tolerant not because free action has moral and religious value, as the Quakers and Milton believed, but because we bracket off our moral and religious beliefs from the rest of our lives and do not let them affect our every-day behavior. As Christopher Hill has said, Locke's "tolerance was the rational calculation of the Toleration Act rather than the humanist idealism of a Milton." Christopher Hill, *The Century of Revolution: 1603-1714* (New York, W.W. Norton & Co., 1980) p. 252. Locke's *Letter Concerning Toleration* probably influenced Jefferson to abandon classical liberal idealism in the case of freedom of religion, and to call for a "wall of separation" between church and state; Jefferson's phrase was incorporated into American constitutional law in *Everson v. Board of Education* (1947).

93. Locke denied authorship of the *Two Treatises* for his entire life, even after the Glorious Revolution made their ideas acceptable. Though he confessed to being its author in his will, while he was alive, he recommended this work to friends as an excellent book on politics by an unknown author. He may just have wanted to avoid controversy, but some historians speculate that he understood that the idea of natural rights in the *Second Treatise* contradicted the empiricism of his famous *Essay concerning Human Understanding*. See Peter Laslett, ed., John

Locke, *Two Treatises of Government* (New York, 1965, New American Library: Mentor Books) p. 15 *et seq.*

94. According to Hume, any statement that tells us about the world had to be based on experience, and a statement can be self-evidently true only if it is a logically necessary tautology that tells us nothing about the world. When Jefferson paraphrased Locke's social contract theory in the Declaration of Independence, saying "We hold these truths to be self-evident, that all men are created equal, that they are endowed with their creator with certain unalienable rights ..., that to secure these rights, governments are instituted among men ..., that whenever any form of government becomes destructive of these ends, it is the right of the people to alter or abolish it ...," he was making a claim that a strict empiricist would dismiss as total nonsense. These "self-evident" statements are not logically necessary: You can deny them without contradicting yourself.

95. Alasdair MacIntyre, *After Virtue* (Notre Dame, Indiana, Notre Dame Press, 1981) is the best account of the inevitable failure of the "Enlightenment project" of developing a rationally based morality free of the older Aristotelian view that nature is teleological. Enlightenment philosophers failed to develop a rational ethics based on natural law, because they accepted the "scientific" view that our knowledge of nature is based on sense experience.

96. Bernard Mandeville, *The Fable of the Bees or Private Vices, Public Benefits* (Oxford, Clarendon Press, 1924).

97. Mill was actually better than his theories and more high-minded than the other utilitarians, even though it led him to self-contradictions. Mill believed in what is called "qualitative hedonism" – that the goal of life is to maximize pleasure, but that there is a hierarchy of pleasures, with some more valuable than others. He said, famously, that "it is better to be Socrates

dissatisfied than a pig satisfied." But this sort of qualitative hedonism contradicts Mill's laissez-faire idea of civil liberties. Laissez-faire assumes that each person knows best what gives him pleasure, so that his free choices maximize his pleasure. If there is a hierarchy of pleasures, then it would make sense to have government discourage people from choosing lower pleasures and encourage them to choose higher pleasures instead. To defend laissez-faire, you must believe in quantitative hedonism, like the other utilitarians. You must believe, as Bentham famously said, that "The quantity of pleasure being equal, push-pin is as good as philosophy."

98. "As for charity, it is a matter in which the immediate effect on the persons directly concerned, and the ultimate consequence to the general good, are apt to be at complete war with one another: while the education given to women – an education of the sentiments rather than of the understanding – and the habit inculcated by their whole life, of looking to immediate effects on persons, and not to remote effects on classes of persons – make them both unable to see, and unwilling to admit, the ultimate evil tendency of any form of charity or philanthropy which commends itself to their sympathetic feelings. The great and continually increasing mass of unenlightened and shortsighted benevolence, which, taking the care of people's lives out of their own hands, and relieving them from the disagreeable consequences of their own acts, saps the very foundations of the self-respect, self-help, and self-control which are the essential conditions both of individual prosperity and of social virtues – this waste of resources and of benevolent feelings in doing harm instead of good, is immensely swelled by women's contributions, and stimulated by their influence." John Stuart Mill, *On the Subjection of Women*, (Greenwich, Conn., Fawcett Premier, 1971) p. 112-113.

99. Frederick the Great is Kant's model in "What is Enlightenment," when he describes the ideal monarch "who is himself enlightened [and] is not afraid of shadows, and who has a well-disciplined army to assure public peace, [who] can say 'Argue as much as you will, and about what you will, only obey!'" Lewis White Beck, ed, *Kant on History* (Indianapolis, Bobbs-Merrill/Library of Liberal Arts, 1963) p. 10.

100. Kant, *Idea for a Universal History*, in Beck, ed, *Kant on History*, p. 22.

101. Kant, *The Metaphysical Elements of Justice*, John Ladd, trans. (Indianapolis, Bobbs-Library/Library of Liberal Arts, 1965) pp. 75-84 and p. 111-114.

102. See Kant, *Perpetual Peace*, in Beck, , ed, *Kant on History*, pp. 111-112. Notice that laws made in this sort of republic are reminiscent of Kant's categorical imperative: When you enact a law in this sort of republic, you are deciding both the maxim that guides your own behavior and the law that guides everyone's behavior.

103. G.W.F. Hegel, *The Philosophy of History*, in Carl J. Friedrich, ed., *The Philosophy of Hegel* (New York, Modern Library, 1954) p. 25.

104. Hegel, *Philosophy of History*, p. 52-53.

105. Francis Fukuyama has confused the issue by writing that there were two nineteenth-century theories of the end of history – Marx's theory that history would end in communism and Hegel's theory that history would end in a liberal state – and that events have proven Hegel right. This is a neat antithesis, but it distorts Hegel's thinking. Hegel believed that history would end in an absolute republican government, where individual will would be completely subordinate to the general will. For example, he says: "What counts in a state is the practice of acting

according to a common will and adopting universal aims. ... particular will has no validity. Whims, lusts are not valid. ... What counts is the common will. In thus being suppressed, the individual will retires into itself. And this is the first condition necessary for the existence of the universal.... Only in this soil, in the state, can art and religion exist. ... The universal Idea manifests itself in the state." *ibid.*, p. 51. Fukuyama writes that Hegel saw the victory of the ideals of the French revolution and of liberal democracy. But the ideal of the French revolution that Hegel actually believed in was Rousseau's ideal republic, where each individual's particular will is totally subordinated to the general will, and this view does not leave any room for the liberal ideal of pluralism – much less for freedom of conscience and civil disobedience.

106. "Lecture on the Times" in *Basic Selections from Emerson*, Eduard C. Lindeman, ed. (New York, Mentor, 1954) p. 29. He states this idealist principle of reform even more forcefully in the "Essay on Human Culture," where he says, "the basis of Culture is that part of human nature which in philosophy is called the Idea. A human being always compares any action or object with somewhat he calls the Perfect: that is to say, not with any action or object now existing in nature, but with a certain Better existing in the mind. That Better, we call the Ideal. Ideal is not opposed to Real but to Actual. The Ideal is the Real. The Actual is but the Apparent and the Temporary. Ideal justice is justice, and not that imperfect, halting compensation which we can attain to by courts and juries." "Human Culture: Introductory" in R. E. Spiller, ed., *Selected Essays, Lectures, and Poems of Ralph Waldo Emerson* (New York, Pocket Books, 1965) p. 117.

107. The movements "for the reform of domestic, civil, literary, and ecclesiastical institutions ... against War, Negro slavery, Usages of trade ... are on all accounts important; they not only check the special abuses, but they educate the conscience and

intellect of the people." Emerson, "Lecture on the Times" in Lindeman, p. 27-28.

108. Emerson, "Politics," in Spiller, p. 323.

109. "The modern mind teaches (in extremes) that the nation exists for the individual; for the guardianship and education of every man. The Reformation contained the new thought, the English Revolution its first expansion. The American Declaration of Independence is a formal announcement of it by a nation to nations though a very limited expression. The Church of Calvin and of the Friends have preached it ever. ... The Vote – universal suffrage – is another [expression of it]; the downfall of war, the attack upon slavery, are others." Emerson, "Human Culture," in Spiller, p. 114.

110. For example, Charles Dickens wrote that Boston was different from the rest of America because "the public institutions and charities of this capital of Massachusetts are as nearly perfect, as the most considerate wisdom, benevolence, and humanity, can make them." Charles Dickens, *American Notes for General Circulation*, John S. Whitley and Arnold Goldman, ed. (Harmondsworth, Middlesex, England, and New York, Penguin Books, 1985, first published 1842) p. 77. He went on to describe charities such as the Perkins Institution and Massachusetts Asylum for the Blind, the State Hospital for the Insane, the Boylston School "for neglected and indigent boys who have committed no crime, but who in the ordinary course of things would very soon be purged of that distinction if they were not taken from the hungry streets and sent here" (p. 99) and the House of Correction "in which silence is strictly maintained, but where the prisoners have the comfort and mental relief of seeing each other, and of working together. This is the improved system of Prison Discipline which we have imported into England, and which has been in successful operation among us for some years past" (p. 100). By contrast, the one institution he describes in

New York city is the Tombs, where prisoners could be kept for up to a year without being let out of their cells for exercise (p. 131), and he finds streets of that city where "Poverty, wretchedness, and vice, are rife ...." (p. 136).

111. Henry James, *The Bostonians* (New York, Signet, 1979) p. 147.

112. Emerson, "The Transcendentalist" in Spiller, p. 103.

113. Emerson, "Works and Days" in Lindeman, p. 122-123.

114. "Things are in the saddle" is from Emerson's "Ode, Inscribed to William H. Channing." "Machinery has been applied to all work and carried to such perfection that little is left for the men but to mind the engines and feed the furnaces But the machines require punctual service and as they never tire they prove too much for their tenders. Mines, forges, mills, breweries, railroads, steam pump, steam plough, drill of regiments, drill of police, rule of court and shop rule have operated to give a mechanical regularity to all the habit and action of men A terrible machine has possessed itself of the ground the air the men and women and hardly even thought is free" is from Emerson's essay "Manners" in R.W. Emerson, Essays and English Traits, (New York, P. Collier and Son: Harvard Classics) p. 381.

115. Henry David Thoreau, *Walden* (New York, New American Library: Mentor Books, 1942) p. 67.

116. Richard Hofstadter, *The American Political Tradition* (New York, Vintage Books, 1959) p. 144.

117. Richard Hofstadter and Walter Metzger, *The Development of Academic Freedom in the United States* (New York, Columbia University Press, 1955) p. 282.

118. Miriam Gurke, *The Ladies of Seneca Falls: The Birth of the Woman's Rights Movement* (New York, Shocken, 1974) p. 243-244.

119. Derek Beales, *From Castelreagh to Gladstone 1815-1885* (London, Sphere Books, 1971) p. 252.

120. Thomas Hill Green, *Lectures on the Principles of Political Obligation* (London, Longmans, 1941) pp. 39-40.

121. James Lincoln Collier, *The Rise of Selfishness in America* (New York, Oxford Univ. Press, 1991) p. 53.

122. Thackeray, *Vanity Fair*, Chapter xlix (New York, Modern Library, undated) p. 551.

123. William Grimes, "Murder! Mayhem! Those were the Days!" *New York Times*, Jan. 26, 1996, p. B1.

124. The radical Democrats in New York city were called the "Locofocos," a common name for friction matches in the early nineteenth century. The Tammany machine had the habit of nominating candidates quickly, and then turning out the gaslights to end the meeting before their opponents could speak. In October, 1835, the radical Democrats brought matches with them to a nominating meeting and used them to light candles when the lights went out, so they could continue the meeting. Schlesinger, *The Age of Jackson*, p. 83-84.

125. Hofstadter, *The American Political Tradition*, p. 170.

126. Hofstadter, *The American Political Tradition*, p. 172.

127. Veblen, *The Engineers and the Price System* (New York, Viking Press, 1954, copyright 1921) p. 121.

128. Oscar Wilde, *The Soul of Man Under Socialism and Other Essays* (New York, Harper & Row, 1970) pp. 227-271.

129. Cited in John Patrick Diggins, *The Rise and Fall of the American Left* (New York, W.W. Norton & Co., 1992, copyright 1973) p. 130.

130. Diggins, *Rise and Fall*, p. 138.

131. Karl Marx and Friedrich Engels, *The Communist Manifesto* (New York and London, Modern Reader Paperbacks, 1964) p. 40.

132. For example, Emerson writes that the reformers of his time "occupy the ground which Calvinism occupied in the last age, and compose the visible church of the existing generation. ... The leaders of the crusades against War, Negro slavery, Usages of trade, Court and Custom-house Oaths, and so on to the agitation on the system of Education and the laws of Property, are the right successors of Luther, Knox, Robinson, Fox, Penn, Wesley, and Whitefield. They have the same virtues and vices; the same noble impulse, and the same bigotry." "Lecture on the Times" in Lindeman, p. 28.

133. The key book that made this point was Adolph Berle and Gardiner Means, *The Modern Corporation and Private Property* (New York, Macmillan, 1933). Berle and Means said that 44 percent of the two-hundred largest American corporations, controlling 58 percent of their wealth, had so many stockholders that their owners had no power over their managers (p. 94). They predicted that more managers would become autonomous as corporations became larger.

134. John Maynard Keynes, "The End of Laissez-Faire" in *Essays in Persuasion* (New York, Harcourt, Brace & Co., 1932) p. 314.

135. John Kenneth Galbraith, *The New Industrial State* (New York, Signet Books, 1968) pp. 33-45 and 83-96.

136. Galbraith, *New Industrial State*, p. 49. Galbraith points out that in 1965, personal savings by individuals were $25 billion, while savings by business firms were $83 billion. Since the early 1950s, personal savings had increased by 50 percent, while business savings had nearly tripled. And only the affluent saved: Households with incomes in the lower two-thirds did no saving

at all. The average person participated in the economy as a consumer, rather than as a saver. p. 48.

137. cited in Christopher Lasch, *The Culture of Narcissism: American Life in an Age of Diminishing Expectations* (New York, W.W. Norton & Co., 1978) p. 77.

138. The term "praxis philosophy" was first used by Habermas. See Jurgen Habermas, *The Philosophical Discourse of Modernity*, Frederick G. Lawrence, trans. (Cambridge, Mass., MIT Press, 1987) p. 60 *et seq*.

139. Alfred Jules Ayers, *Language, Truth and Logic* (New York, Dover, 1952) is the best statement of the logical positivists' ideas on ethics.

140. In his technical work on the scientific method, Popper criticized the logical positivists themselves for being too dogmatic. The positivists had claimed that scientists could *verify* hypotheses through experiments, but Popper said that experiments could only *falsify* hypotheses. He said that science is critical – scientists advance theories and invent experiments to disprove them – and the logical positivists themselves were going too far when they claimed that science could find the truth. Yet scientific theories are more reliable than other forms of thought, because they are developed through this critical, experimental process.

141. Karl R. Popper, *The Open Society and Its Enemies* (Princeton, N.J., Princeton University Press, 1966) vol. 2, pp. 82-83.

142. Popper, *The Open Society*, vol. 1, p. 22.

143. Popper, *The Open Society*, vol. 1, p. 23.

144. Popper, *The Open Society*, vol. 1, pp. 58-59.

145. Popper, *The Open Society*, vol. 1, pp. 157-159.

146. John Dewey, *Individualism Old and New* (New York, Capricorn Books, 1962, copyright 1929, 1930) p. 95.

147. Dewey, *Individualism*, pp. 119-120.

148. Dewey, *Individualism*, p. 117.

149. John Dewey, *Reconstruction in Philosophy* (New York, New American Library: Mentor Books, 1950) p. 131.

150. Dewey, *Reconstruction*, p. 136.

151. Dewey, *Reconstruction*, p. 138 -139. He sums up this point by saying, "Reason, always an honorific term in ethics, becomes actualized in the methods by which the needs and conditions, the obstacles and resources, of situations are scrutinized in detail, and intelligent plans of improvement are worked out" p. 140. That is, ethical reasoning should deal only with means, not with ends.

152. Dewey, *Reconstruction*, p. 141.

153. Daniel Bell, *The End of Ideology: On the Exhaustion of Political Ideas in the Fifties* (Glencoe, Illinois, The Free Press, 1960).

154. Freud himself began to admit this later in his life and wrote: "My self-knowledge tells me I have never really been a doctor in the proper sense. It still strikes me, myself, as strange that the case histories I write should read like short stories and that, as one might say, they lack the serious stamp of science." In fact, Freud was nominated for the Nobel Prize in literature, and the novelist Thomas Mann endorsed the nomination. More recently, Alan Stone, Professor of Psychiatry at Harvard, argued in a lecture to the American Academy of Psychoanalysis that, as psychology becomes more scientific and biological, we can appreciate Freud only if we recognize that his work belongs to the arts and humanities, rather than the sciences. See Michael

Kimmelman, "Matter Over Mind: A Freudian Trove," *New York Times*, April 16, 1999, p. B29.

155. Karl Marx and Frederick Engels, *The German Ideology*, R. Pacal, ed. (New York, International Publishers, 1947) p. 79 *et seq.*

156. David Lehman, *Signs of the Times: Deconstruction and the Fall of Paul De Man* (New York, Simon & Schuster: Poseidon Press, 1991) p. 58.

157. Lehman, *Signs*, p. 35.

158. On crime, see Foucault, *Discipline and Punish*. On madness, see Foucault, *Madness and Civilization*. Likewise, in *The History of Sexuality*, Foucault argues that there is no such thing as a homosexual – heterosexuality and homosexuality are nothing more than categories imposed by power, beginning with the Christians' attempt to suppress sexuality and continuing in the psychotherapists' attempt to classify sexuality so they could treat it. The pre-Christian Greeks did not identify themselves as homosexual or heterosexual, and so they were able to enjoy both forms of sexuality.

159. For example, see Ian Taylor and Laurie Taylor, *Politics and Deviance* (New York, Penguin, 1973).

160. "What, then, is the postmodern? ... It is undoubtedly a part of the modern. All that has been received, if only yesterday ... must be suspected." Jean-Francois Lyotard, "What is Post-Modernism?" in *The Postmodern Condition: A Report on Knowledge*, Geoff Bennington and Brian Massumi, trans. (Minneapolis, University of Minnesota Press, 1984) p. 79.

161. Bruno Bettelheim pointed out that the Nazis were the first to have courses in Ethnic Studies – *Rassenwissenschaft* in German – which focused on the history and the "perspectives" of one race, rather than focusing on a body of knowledge, regardless of the race of the scholar. See Bruno Bettelheim, *Obsolete Youth*

(San Francisco, San Francisco Press, 1970) p. 4. Bettelheim was sensitive to this issue as a psychoanalyst who had been practicing in Germany when the Nazis gained power. The Nazis attacked psychoanalysis because it was a "Jewish science" that did not belong in an Aryan country, rather than because it was untrue. This essay originally appeared in *Encounter* magazine in 1969, and unfortunately, it was heavily edited when it was included in Bruno Bettelheim, *Surviving: And Other Essays* (New York, Random House: Vintage Books, 1980).

162. cited by Christopher Lasch, *The True and Only Heaven: Progress and its Critics* (New York, W.W. Norton & Co, 1991) p. 395.

163. "Letter from a Birmingham Jail" in Martin Luther King, Jr., *Why We Can't Wait* (New York, New American Library: Signet Books, 1964) p. 82.

164. Lasch, *True and Only Heaven*, pp. 399-407.

165. "the controversy surrounding the Moynihan report had the effect of curtailing serious research on minority problems in the inner city for over a decade, as liberal scholars shied away from researching behavior construed as unflattering or stigmatizing to particular racial minorities." William Julius Wilson, *The Truly Disadvantaged: The Inner City, the Underclass, and Public Policy* (Chicago and London, Chicago University Press, 1990) p. 4.

166. cited in cited in Gertrude Himmelfarb, *The De-moralization of Society: From Victorian Virtues to Modern Values* (New York, Vintage Books, 1996) p. 241.

167. The ACLU did have historic connections with Bohemian socialism: Before Roger Baldwin founded the ACLU, he cofounded the Civil Liberties Bureau with Crystal Eastman, the sister of Max Eastman, editor of *The Masses*, to protect leftists and pacifists from censorship during World War I; one of this

group's cases was to defend pacifist articles in *The Masses* from censorship. But the repression during and after World War I ended Bohemian socialism and was a real threat to free speech. For example, the Espionage Act of 1917 made it a crime to obstruct the effort to enlist men in the army, and the Justice Department held that any criticism of the war would influence men not to enlist. The 1918 Sedition Act went further by outlawing any abusive language about the government of the United States; under this law, Eugene V. Debs was sentenced to ten years in prison for a speech opposing the general idea of war. Beginning in 1917, the U.S. Postal Service denied second class mailing privileges to the entire anti-war and socialist press, including *The Masses*. The ACLU played a prominent role in defending the First Amendment from these threats to political speech. Samuel Walker, *In Defense of American Liberties: A History of the ACLU* (New York, Oxford University Press, 1990) pp. 11-14. The political climate remained so repressive through the 1950s that the ACLU had to focus on defending political speech and other serious speech.

168. In *Everson*, the Court incorporated the phrase "wall of separation between church and state" into its interpretation of the Constitution, because this phrase had been used in a letter from Jefferson to Madison about the struggle to disestablish the Episcopal Church in Virginia. The Court reasoned that, because this debate occurred shortly before Jefferson and Madison played a major role in the adoption of the Bill of Rights, this letter expressed the intention of the founders. However, more recent scholarship, which Justice Rehnquist drew on in his dissent to *Wallace v. Jaffree* (1985), shows that the debate in the First Congress implied that there should not be a "wall of separation" between church and state. The Founders' generation believed that liberty was more secure if religion flourished, and so they believed in public accommodation of the religious beliefs of the American people and in government providing non-

discriminatory support for religious institutions to achieve legitimate government ends. Most government practice and legal theory for over a century after the ratification of the First Amendment reflects these beliefs.

169. In *Lynch v. Donelly* (1984) the ACLU suffered what it considered a major defeat in its efforts to stop Christmas displays on public property, which it made the subject of annual lawsuits. Chief Justice Burger's opinion held that Pawtucket, Rhode Island, could display a crèche on public property, but only because it was celebrating the historical origins of a secular holiday, rather than promoting a religious point of view; the Court held it was not a religious display, because the crèche was surrounded by a clown, an elephant, a teddy bear, Santa's workshop, and a wishing well. In *Allegheny County v. ACLU* (1989), the Court rejected the ACLU's challenge to a display that included a Chanukah menorah and a sign saluting liberty, as well as a Christmas tree; in this case, the court refused to allow a crèche on public property, because it was not surrounded by other toys, as it had been in the 1984 case, making it an explicitly religious symbol whose display on public property constituted establishment of religion. This standard is sometimes called the "three plastic animals" rule. In 1995, however, the Supreme Court ruled that a crèche on public property is legal as long as it is erected by a private group and the property is a public forum that is equally accessible to the speech of all private groups – the first time in many years that this sort of religious speech was not specially handicapped.

170. In one of their fund-raising mailings, the ACLU made this astounding statement: "[conservatives] claim that students and others do not have the right to pray in public places. But that's not true. All of us can pray privately whenever and wherever we choose. But, if you are a teacher in a public school or leading a public school ceremony, for example, the Supreme Court has

ruled that you can't make everyone else share your personal prayer with you." How would the ACLU react if the Supreme Court applied this rule to any other First Amendment right – for example, if it ruled that teachers and students can think privately about their political opinions in the public schools but cannot make everyone else share those personal thoughts by saying them out loud? Obviously, conservatives do not really claim that people are forbidden to say private prayers in their own minds in public places; they claim that people are forbidden to pray publicly.

171. *Coates v. City of Cincinnati* (1971) struck down an ordinance that prohibited three or more persons gathering on a sidewalk and annoying passersby, on First Amendment grounds, as a violation of freedom of assembly and freedom of speech (because the word "annoying" is overbroad, and could also be used to stop a political speech if a passerby said that it annoyed him). But cities responded by passing anti-loitering laws that do not mention any number of people: any activity that is illegal for one person is also illegal for a group of people.

172. After *Papachristou v. City of Jacksonville* struck down anti-loitering laws on the grounds of vagueness, loitering plus laws defined the illegal behavior much more precisely: For example, a law against loitering with the intent to sell drugs might make it illegal to stand on the street for more than fifteen minutes, and to have at least one contact with another person that lasts less than two minutes, and to transfer a small object to another person, and so on.

173. Courts in California, Colorado, Massachusetts, New Jersey, Oregon and Washington have ruled that shopping centers are public places, where there should be some protection for freedom of speech. In the other states, the move from Main Streets to shopping centers has reduced freedom of speech: In fact, because most people shop at shopping centers, it has

blocked the best opportunity that small groups had for political campaigning.

174. In a speech in New Orleans, Bill Clinton said that he supported a curfew on that city's model: youths under 17 are not allowed out after 8 PM on weekdays (9 PM during the summer), except those who are going to or from work or supervised activities. *San Francisco Chronicle*, May 31, 1996, p. 1. New Orleans adopted the curfew in 1995, and armed robbery by young people dropped by 33 percent in the following year. But this is the most stringent curfew of any major city in the country, and it was only adopted because New Orleans had much worse crime than most cities. More typical is the San Jose, California, curfew of 10 PM for those under 15 and 11:30 PM for those under 17, which caused juvenile crime to drop 12 percent in less than a year. Teenage loitering laws make more sense than curfews: Most people would not want to prevent young people from visiting friends or going to other unsupervised activities after 8 PM, as New Orleans does, but most people also would not want young people hanging out on street corners after 8 PM.

175. Amitai Etzioni, *The Spirit of Community: Rights, Responsibilities, and the Communitarian Agenda* (New York, Crown Publishers, 1993) p. 184.

176. Threats to serious speech remained common through the McCarthy era. McCarthyites prosecuted Communist party officials under the Smith Act, which made it illegal to advocate violent overthrow of the government. After *Yates v. United States* (1957) and *Scales v. United States* (1961), prosecutions under the Smith Act virtually ceased.

177. Walker, *In Defense of American Liberties*, p. 234.

178. Obscenity law was very unsettled for a time: Between 1957, when the Court announced its first obscenity standard in *Roth v. United States*, and 1973, when it announced the current

obscenity standard in *Miller v. California*, there was no case where five justices agreed on what standard distinguishes obscenity from protected speech. Despite the disagreements, the Court effectively ended obscenity prosecutions between 1967 and 1971 by reversing thirty-one obscenity convictions. Liberals were sure that obscenity laws would be overturned completely, but in *Miller* (1973), the more conservative Burger court did develop an obscenity standard – with four liberal justices dissenting. Chief Justice Burger's opinion set up a three-pronged test for obscenity: the average person, applying contemporary community standards must find that the work as a whole appeals to prurient interest; the work must depict or describe sexual content specifically defined by state law; and the work taken as a whole must lack any serious literary, artistic, or political value. Yet the Court has been reluctant to rule that any actual expression is obscene under this standard, so most sexually explicit material is now protected in fact if not in theory.

179. Charles Rembar, *The End of Obscenity*, NY, Bantam Books, 1969, p. 10.

180. In the United States, communities have only a very limited right to regulate pornography. For example, New York City has implemented a zoning plan that has improved Times Square by shifting sex shops that sell pornographic books and movies to industrial districts adjoining the city's outlying neighborhoods. The residents of these neighborhoods have complained, but under the current interpretation of the First Amendment, the city cannot ban sex shops outright. New York's plan is based on *Renton v. Playtime Theaters* (1986), where a conservative Supreme Court upheld a zoning law that prohibited adult movie theaters within 1,000 feet of residential zones, churches, parks and schools, on the grounds that this regulation served a legitimate government purpose without suppressing the content of the speech.

181. *Whitney v. California*, 274 U.S. 357, 375 (1927).

182. It is interesting to compare Voltaire's view of speech with the modernist view. Voltaire wrote neo-classical dramas that did not allow any violence on stage: He called Shakespeare a barbarian, because he let his audience see characters stabbing each other rather than having a messenger describe their death. Modernists hate this sort of censorship of artistic expression – even if it is self-censorship, like Voltaire's – and they admire writers like Artaud, Genet and Burroughs who break through this sort of barrier. But, unlike the modernists, Voltaire and his contemporaries also believed that we can reason about whether our behavior and our social arrangements are right or wrong, so Voltaire's writing was genuinely dangerous to the people in power: He was censored and driven out of France, because the king and church knew they would lose their power if people were convinced that his ideas were true. If we accept the modernist view, speech can never threaten the established social order in this way: Speech-as-action can subvert conventional behavior and open up new areas for personal freedom, but it cannot tell us how the public world should be governed.

183. In 1984, the Supreme Court struck down an law based on this theory, which banned pornography as a form of sex discrimination that degrades women. The law, supported by feminists and opposed by the ACLU, was struck down in *American Booksellers Association, Inc., v. Hudnut*, and the ruling was summarily affirmed by the Supreme Court.

184. For example, see *Doe v. Michigan* (1989), *UWM Post v. Board of Regents of University of Wisconsin* (1991), and *Corry v. Stanford* (1995).

185. Ivan Illich, *Medical Nemesis: The Expropriation of Health* (New York, Pantheon, 1976).

186. From the editorial "Curfews and Common Sense" in the *New York Times*, June 11, 1996, p. A14: "Curfews are but a short-term fix to deeper problems.... The sensible and lasting solutions to teen-age crime are better schools, stronger families and well-financed, community-based recreational and remedial programs." The *Times* apparently believes that well-financed recreational programs are not just a short-term fix for deeper problems: If only we spent enough money on recreational programs, we would get at the deepest socio-psychological causes of crime.

187. In 1900, America's per capita income was $3838 in 1992 dollars. Bureau of the Census, *Historical Statistics of the United States: Colonial Times to 1970* (Washington, DC, 1975) p. 224, converted to 1992 dollars. This is just above what we now define as the poverty line, which is $3583 in 1992 dollars per person in a family of four.

188. In 1900, America's per capita GDP was $5,557 in 2005 dollars. In 2000, America's per capita GDP was $39,750 in 2005 dollars. Louis D. Johnston and Samuel H. Williamson, "The Annual Real and Nominal GDP for the United States, 1790 - Present," Measuring Worth, 2008. www.measuringworth.org.

189. Ronald Inglehart, *Modernization and Postmodernization: Cultural, Economic and Political Change in 43 Societies* (Princeton, NJ, Princeton University Press, 1997) p. 28 *et seq.*

190. The research is summarized in James Gustave Speth, *The Bridge at the End of the World: Capitalism, the Environment, and Crossing from Crisis to Sustainability* (New Haven and London, Yale University Press, 2008) pp. 129-134.

191. Charles Siegel, *The Politics of Simple Living* (Berkeley, CA: Preservation Institute, 2008) and Charles Siegel, *The Preservationist Manifesto* (Berkeley, CA, Northbrae Books, 1995).

192. John Maynard Keynes, "Economic Possibilities for Our Grandchildren" in *Essays in Persuasion* (New York, Harcourt Brace & Co., 1932) p. 365-367.

193. Benjamin Kline Hunnicutt, *Work Without End: Abandoning Shorter Hours for the Right to Work* (Philadelphia, Temple University Press, 1988).

194. See Juliet B. Schor, "Can the North Stop Consumption Growth? Escaping the Cycle of Work and Spend" in V. Bhaskar and Andrew Glyn, ed., *The North, the South and the Environment: Ecological Constraints and the Global Economy* (New York, St. Martin's Press, 1995) pp. 68-84 and Juliet B. Schor, *Plenitude: The New Economics of True Wealth* (Penguin Press HC, 2010).

195. Juliet Schor, *The Overworked American: The Unexpected Decline of Leisure* (New York, Basic Books, 1991) p. 133.

196. One survey of male heads of households found that 85 percent said they had no choice of work hours. Another survey of married men found that 85 percent had to work hours they would not choose in order to keep their jobs. Schor, *The Overworked American*, p. 128.

197. In 2009, the average Dutch worker worked 1,288 hours per year, and the average American worker worked 1,776 hours per year. Organization for Economic Cooperation and Development, "Average annual hours actually worked per worker" OECD Stat Extracts, http://stats.oecd.org/Index.aspx?DataSetCode=ANHRS.

198. Peter Victor, Managing Without Growth: Slower by Design, not Disaster (Edward Elgar Publishing, 2008).

199. Schor, "Can the North Stop Consumption Growth" pp. 68-84.

200. See Ronald Inglehart, *Culture Shift in Advanced Industrial Society* (Princeton, N.J., Princeton University Press, 1990) and Inglehart, *Modernization and Postmodernization*, pp. 108-159. For the figure for the Netherlands in comparison with figures for other countries, see *Modernization and Postmodernization*, p. 157.

201. Benjamin Kline Hunnicutt, *Kellogg's Six-Hour Day* (Philadelphia, Temple University Press, 1996) p. 10.

202. Hunnicutt, *Kellogg's Six-Hour Day*, pp. 169-76.

203. Health-care costs rose dramatically after Medicare was adopted in 1965, to pay for health care for the elderly. In order to buy off doctors who were opposed to this new form of "socialized medicine," Medicare extended coverage to all doctor bills as well as to all hospital bills. Before this time, most health insurance covered only hospital bills, which ordinary people could not pay, and not doctors' bills, which most people could pay for themselves; but after 1965, most health plans imitated Medicare, extending the cost-plus method of payment to cover all the medical bills of most Americans.

204. Illich, *Medical Nemesis*, p. 112.

205. See Michael M. Weinstein, "Curbing the High Cost of Health Care," *New York Times*, July 29, 2001, "Week In Review" section.

206. John C. Goodman and Gerald L. Musgrave, *Patient Power: The Free-Enterprise Alternative to Clinton's Health Plan* (Washington, D.C., Cato Institute, 1994).

207. Pam Belluck, "Obesity Rates Hit Plateau in U.S., Data Suggest," *New York Times*, January 13, 2010.

208. Catarina Saraiva and Michael Quint, "Paterson-Backed Sugary Beverage Tax Is 'Unfair,' Opponents Say." *Business Week*, March 08, 2010.

209. From 1959 through 1974, spending per student increased by 4.7 percent a year in real terms, more than a percentage point greater than GNP growth. Robert Reich, *The Work of Nations*, p. 255. After 15 years of growth at that rate, we spent more than twice as much per student – yet achievement declined.

210. In 1963 and 1964, SAT scores averaged 478 on the verbal portion and 502 on the mathematical portion. They declined until 1980, when verbal scores reached 424 and mathematical scores 466. Math scores rose after 1980 to 482 in 1995, but verbal scores have only risen to 428. Beginning in 1996, the College Board "recentered" its scoring methods to accommodate today's lower levels of achievement. Diane Ravitch, "Defining Literacy Downward," *New York Times*, August 28, 1996, p. A15.

211. James S. Coleman et al., *Equality of Educational Opportunity* (Washington, D.C., U. S. Government Printing Office, 1966) concludes that "When these [socioeconomic] factors are statistically controlled, however, it appears that differences between schools account for only a small fraction of differences in pupil achievement" (pp. 21-22). Christopher Jencks et al., *Inequality: A Reassessment of the Effect of Family and Schooling in America* (New York, Basic Books, 1972) concludes that "qualitative differences between schools also have relatively little effect on students' eventual educational attainment" (p. 146) and that "We have shown that the most important determinant of educational attainment is family background. ... Except for family background, the most important determinant of educational attainment is probably cognitive skill. ... Qualitative differences between high schools

seem to explain about 2 percent of the variation in students' educational attainment." (pp. 158-159).

212. Eric A. Hanushek, "The Impact of Differential Expenditures on School Performance," *Educational Researcher*, May 1989, pp. 45-50. After reviewing 187 studies, Hanushek concluded "There is no strong or systematic relationship between school expenditures and student performance" (p. 47). For example, of 152 studies that examined the effect of class size on achievement, 125 did not show statistically significant differences in achievement in classes of different sizes, 14 showed higher achievement in smaller classes, and 13 showed higher achievement in larger classes. Studies that examined the effect of higher expenditures on teacher salaries, facilities, and administration had similar results. However, Hanushek adds, studies have shown that teachers and schools that use different teaching methods do differ in their effectiveness; it is only the easily measurable indexes of educational quality used in most studies, such as spending per pupil and student-teacher ratio, that have no effect (p. 48).

213. Lawrence Steinberg, *Beyond the Classroom: Why School Reform has Failed and What Parents Need to Do* (New York, Simon & Schuster, 1996) p. 50.

214. A study of twenty-one OECD nations found that the United States spent more per public school student than any other country studied, about $6,010 per student annually compared with an average of $4,180 for all countries studied. Yet another OECD study done at about the same time concluded that the United States elementary and secondary schools were mediocre. Chester E. Finn, Jr., "Will They Ever Learn?" *National Review*, May 29, 1995, p. 28.

215. Sara McLanahan and Gary Sandefur, *Growing Up with a Single Parent: What Hurts, What Helps* (Cambridge, Mass, Harvard University Press, 1994) p. 42.

216. McLanahan and Sandefur, *Growing Up with a Single Parent*, p. 49.

217. McLanahan and Sandefur, *Growing Up with a Single Parent*, pp. 53-4. This figure applies to women born after 1953. They also found that these children's problems are not just caused by poverty. Though the poverty rate for families headed by single parents is 26.5 percent, compared with just 5.3 percent for families headed by two parents (p. 82), the damage caused by poverty accounts for only about half of their disadvantage compared with children from intact families (pp. 79-95). And when divorced parents remarry, they regain ground economically, but their children are no better off than children of divorced parents who do not remarry.

218. For the best summary of the research, see David Popenoe, *Life Without Father: Compelling New Evidence that Fatherhood and Marriage are Indispensable for the Good of Children and Society* (New York, Free Press, 1996), particularly pp. 52-78. Another good summary of the research is in Barbara Dafoe Whitehead, "Dan Quail Was Right" *The Atlantic*, April, 1993, p. 47 et seq. See also Barbara Dafoe Whitehead, *The Divorce Culture* (New York, Alfred A. Knopf: Distributed by Random House, 1997) and David Blankenhorn, *Fatherless America: Confronting our Most Urgent Social Problem* (New York, Basic Books, 1995).

219. William R. Mattox, Jr., "The Parent Trap," *Policy Review*, No. 55, Winter 1991, p. 6.

220. For example, a 1995 study by the Families and Work Institute shows that only 15 percent of working women with school-age children want to work full time, although 75 percent

currently do so. Sylvia Ann Hewlett and Cornel West, *The War Against Parents* (Boston, Houghton Mifflin, 1998) p. 107.

221. In 1900, 95 percent of married women did not work; virtually all of the 5 percent who did work were either black women in domestic service or immigrants working at factory jobs, which shows that only the poorest of the poor could not afford to care for their own children. Sar A. Levitan, Richard S. Belous, and Frank Gallo, *What's Happening to the American Family?: Tensions, Hopes, Realities*, revised edition (Baltimore and London, Johns Hopkins Press, 1988) p. 85.

222. "... significant headway has been made in the field of biology, where researchers have begun to grasp how the brain develops. ... Dr. Frank Goodwin, former director of the National Institute of Mental Health, cites studies in which children who could be described as being 'at risk' for developmental problems were exposed at an early age to a stimulating environment. ... At the age of four months, half of the children were placed in a preschool with a very high ratio of adult staff to children. ... those in the experimental group averaged 17 points higher in IQ tests." Hillary Clinton, *It Takes a Village: And Other Lessons Children Teach Us* (New York, Simon & Schuster: Touchstone Books, 1996) pp. 56-61. Clinton exaggerates the benefits of these programs. For example, though IQ initially increases by 17 points, the gain diminishes over time and is less than 5 points by the time the children reach high school – not enough to make a significant difference in school achievement. John T. Bruer, *The Myth of the First Three Years : A New Understanding of Early Brain Development and Lifelong Learning* (New York, Free Press, 1999) p 171. Though children who were in day care have higher scores than the control group of poor, at-risk children who did not go to day care, they still have much lower scores than the national average: The Abecedarian Project is one of the most widely admired examples of the benefits of preschools with

enriched environments, but the poor, at-risk children that it enrolled still did much worse than the average American child, though they did better than the control group of poor at-risk children who stayed home. For example, 30 percent of the children in the Abecedarian program had to repeat a year in school, compared with 56 percent of those who stayed home, still far worse than the average middle-class child. Yet constant repetition has convinced middle-class parents that their children's brains would also be hard-wired to make them more intelligent if they were in day care during the first three years of their lives.

223. For more details, see Charles Siegel, *What's Wrong with Day Care: Freeing Parents to Raise their Own Children* (New York, Teachers College Press, 2001) p. 47 *et seq.*

224. See Siegel, *What's Wrong with Day Care*, p. 51 *et seq.*

225. As published in the *Atlanta Journal-Constitution*, March 18, 2001.

226. John de Graaf, David Wann, Thomas H. Naylor, *Affluenza: The All-Consuming Epidemic* (San Francisco, BerrettKoehler, 2002) p. 78.

227. David Cay Johnston, "Income Gap Is Widening, Data Shows," *New York Times*, March 29, 2007, pp. C1 and C10.

228. "Obama Criticizes Campaign Finance Ruling." CNN Political Ticker. Turner Broadcasting System, Inc. 2010-01-20. http://politicalticker.blogs.cnn.com/2010/01/21/obama-criticizes-campaign-finance-ruling.

229. Superville, Darlene (2010-01-23). "President Blasts Supreme Court Over Citizens United Decision." The Huffington Post. http://www.huffingtonpost.com/2010/01/23/obama-weekly-address-vide_n_434082.html.

230. "There may easily be a greater quantity of any particular commodity than is desired by those who have the desire to purchase, and it is abstractly conceivable that this might be the case for all commodities. The error is in not perceiving that though all who have an equivalent to give *might* be fully provided with every consumable article which they desire, the fact that they go on adding to production proves that this is not actually the case." Thus, once workers "had no further desire for necessaries or luxuries, they would take the benefit of any further increase in wages by diminishing their work, so that the overproduction which then for the first time would be possible in idea, could not even then take place in fact, for want of labourers." John Stuart Mill, *Principles of Political Economy* in *Collected Works*, vol 3, J.M. Robson, editor (Toronto, University of Toronto Press, and London, Routledge & Kegan Paul, 1965) pp. 572 and 573-574.

231. Aristotle, *Nichomachean Ethics*, Book X, Chapter 7.

232. Hobbes, *Leviathan*, Part I, Chapter xi.

233. as quoted earlier.

234. as quoted earlier.

235. Isaiah Berlin, *Two Concepts of Liberty: An Inaugural Lecture Delivered Before the University of Oxford on 31 October 1958* (Oxford, Clarendon Press, 1958).

236. Berlin acknowledges that T.H. Green was a true liberal, though Green believed in positive freedom, but he does not mention why Green criticized laissez-faire: Green said that factory workers are less free if the market forces them to work in dangerous and degraded conditions, and Berlin never grapples with this fact.

237. "With *West Virginia v. Barnette*, the procedural republic had arrived." Sandel, *Democracy's Discontent*, p. 54.

238. For example, see Milton's sonnet, "On the new forcers of Conscience under the Long Parliament."

239. Mary Ann Glendon, *Rights Talk*. Glendon makes this point throughout the book. For example, she admires the Universal Declaration of Human Rights, because it says the rights it lists may be limited to secure "the just requirements of morality, public order, and the general welfare ..." (p. 13), she admires the European convention on human rights because, after guaranteeing the right to privacy, it says that governments may interfere with this right "in the interests of national security, public safety or the economic well-being of the country, for the prevention of disorder or crime, for the protection of health and morals ..." (p. 147), and she admires the Canadian charter of rights because "Like most postwar constitutions, the Charter has avoided hard-edged, American-style proclamations of individual rights. The rights it protects are subject to a variety of express limitations, and some are subject to legislative override" (p. 167).